Juárez

Wisconsin/Warner Bros. Screenplay Series

Juárez

Edited with an introduction by

Paul J. Vanderwood

Published for the Wisconsin Center for Film and Theater Research by
The University of Wisconsin Press

Published 1983

The University of Wisconsin Press
114 North Murray Street
Madison, Wisconsin 53715

The University of Wisconsin Press, Ltd.
1 Gower Street
London WC1E 6HA, England

First printing

Printed in the United States of America

For LC CIP information see the colophon

ISBN 0-299-08740-9 cloth; 0-299-08744-1 paper

Publication of this volume has been assisted by a grant from
The Brittingham Fund, Inc.

Contents

Foreword 7
Tino Balio

Introduction: A Political Barometer 9
Paul J. Vanderwood

Illustrations 42

Juárez 57

Notes to the Screenplay 249

Production Credits 256

Cast 257

Inventory 259

Foreword

In donating the Warner Film Library to the Wisconsin Center for Film and Theater Research in 1969, along with the RKO and Monogram film libraries and UA corporate records, United Artists created a truly great resource for the study of American film. Acquired by United Artists in 1957, during a period when the major studios sold off their films for use on television, the Warner library is by far the richest portion of the gift, containing eight hundred sound features, fifteen hundred short subjects, nineteen thousand still negatives, legal files, and press books, in addition to screenplays for the bulk of the Warner Brothers product from 1930 to 1950. For the purposes of this project, the company has granted the Center whatever publication rights it holds to the Warner films. In so doing, UA has provided the Center another opportunity to advance the cause of film scholarship.

Our goal in publishing these Warner Brothers screenplays is to explicate the art of screenwriting during the thirties and forties, the so-called Golden Age of Hollywood. In preparing a critical introduction and annotating the screenplay, the editor of each volume is asked to cover such topics as the development of the screenplay from its source to the final shooting script, differences between the final shooting script and the release print, production information, exploitation and critical reception of the film, its historical importance, its directorial style, and its position within the genre. He is also encouraged to go beyond these guidelines to incorporate supplemental information concerning the studio system of motion picture production.

We could set such an ambitious goal because of the richness of the script files in the Warner Film Library. For many film titles, the files might contain the property (novel, play, short story, or original story idea), research materials, variant drafts of scripts (from story outline to treatment to shooting script), post-production items such as press books and dialogue continuities, and legal records (details of the acquisition of the property, copyright registration, and contracts with actors and directors). Editors of the Wisconsin/Warner Bros. Screenplay Series receive copies of all the materials, along with prints of the films (the most authoritative ones available for reference purposes), to use in preparing the introductions and annotating the final shooting scripts.

In the process of preparing the screenplays for publication, typographical errors were corrected, punctuation and capitalization were modernized, and the format was redesigned to facilitate readability.

Unless otherwise specified, the photographs are frame enlargements taken from a 35-mm print of the film provided by United Artists.

In 1977 Warner Brothers donated the company's production records and distribution records to the University of Southern California and Princeton University, respectively. These materials are now available to researchers and complement the contents of the Warner Film Library donated to the Center by United Artists.

Tino Balio
General Editor

Introduction: *A Political Barometer*

Paul J. Vanderwood

World tensions, presidential politics, and Warner Brothers' profits spawned and shaped the motion picture *Juárez*. Framed loosely within the historically dramatic imperial French invasion of Mexico, the movie pits Mexico's allegedly democratic, pure-blooded Zapotec Indian president, Benito Juárez, against the well-intentioned, but decidedly royalist Austrian couple, Maximilian and Carlotta. Within this concept the film aimed to settle the major international question of its day: which would prevail, democracy or dictatorship? And it meant to teach the kind of steadfastness and hemispheric solidarity that the United States preached as necessary to repel European totalitarianism in this region of the world. Moviemakers in the 1930s were discouraged by their industry from making pointedly political pictures; such movies were considered to be too controversial and opposed to public taste. But *Juárez* meant to cut against that grain. It was supposed to be ideologically clear-cut, but in fact the story line and imagery blurred political differences between the major antagonists, and the picture seriously suffered as it catered to the public and private demands of its time.

Militant European fascism in search of western hemispheric sympathies in 1937 broke surface in Latin America, as the Nazis sought support for the Anti-Comintern Pact that Germany had just signed with Italy and Japan. Fascist organizations found allies in countries where the concept of dictatorship was not entirely foreign and resentment toward "Yankee imperialism" great. German and Italian agents established new military missions in the region, underwrote the sales of weapons, set up propaganda outlets, controlled several airlines, and strengthened trade links to their dictatorships. European-styled fascists called Integralists unsuccessfully attempted to overthrow the Brazilian government, but fascist influence still remained powerful and widespread in Latin America. Hermann Goering had earlier ordered the German aircraft industry to produce transatlantic planes, and reports circulated that Germany had two thousand planes that could reach South America from Africa.[1]

Although many North Americans were concerned about the rise of German power in the middle 1930s and the corresponding decline of British and French ability to preserve a balance in Europe, their isolationist stance was not shaken. Not many believed war would envelop Europe, and, besides, concerns over the Depression at home came first. President Franklin D. Roosevelt tried to help Europe avoid war, but at the same time he was determined to keep up his country's guard. As the battleground broadened—the Japanese showed an appetite for post-Manchurian adventures in the Far East, the Italians invaded Ethiopia, Spain erupted in civil war, and Hitler's posture toward his neighbors became more arrogant—both Roosevelt and the American public stiffened their stance toward international aggression. Neutrality prevailed and people still resisted active involvement in European and Asian quarrels, but the nation's determination grew to defend the Western Hemisphere as the last bastion of democracy. Speaking in Canada in mid-1938, Roosevelt warned the Nazis that aggression in the New World would find the hemisphere united.[2]

This plea for unity among American nations represented an extension of the Good Neighbor Policy, which the president had

1. William L. Langer and S. Everett Gleason, *The Challenge to Isolation: 1937–1940* (New York: Harper and Row, 1952), pp. 40–42; Allan Nevins, *The New Deal and World Affairs: A Chronicle of International Affairs, 1933–1945* (New Haven: Yale University Press, 1950), pp. 166–67; Alton Frye, *Nazi Germany and the American Hemisphere, 1933–1941* (New Haven: Yale University Press, 1967), pp. 101, 174–75, 192; Robert Dallek, *Franklin D. Roosevelt and American Foreign Policy: 1932–1945* (New York: Oxford University Press, 1979), pp. 132–34.

2. Langer and Gleason, *Challenge to Isolation*, pp. 11–12, 40; Phillip E. Jacob, "Influence of World Events on U.S. 'Neutrality' Opinion," *Public Opinion Quarterly*, March 1940, pp. 48, 64–65; Nevins, *New Deal*, pp. 159–60.

launched in his inaugural address, whereby the United States, in search of a new cooperation among the American states, swore off intervention in the internal and external affairs of other hemispheric nations. Latin reaction to the new policy varied from suspicion to contempt, while North American foreign policy planners themselves argued over the intent and application of the new measure. Roosevelt steadfastly opposed direct U.S. intervention in Latin America for any reason; his priority was to revive seriously flagging U.S. trade to the south, and at his insistence the United States in 1933 supported a noninterference declaration adopted at the Inter-American Conference in Montevideo, Uruguay.[3]

Further deterioration of European peace reinforced FDR's determination to strengthen hemispheric relations, and in 1936 he called for a conference in Buenos Aires, Argentina, to explore means of safeguarding the Americas against outside totalitarian penetration. The president himself attended the December conclave, where the public and delegates received him as a hero. He did not get the binding accord he sought from the meeting, but the diplomats agreed at least to consult one another when hemispheric security seemed endangered. On his return to the United States, Roosevelt warned that the "possible attack has been brought infinitely closer than it was five years, or twenty years, or fifty years ago." And at the Inter-American Conference of 1938 in Lima, Peru, the American republics agreed for the first time to share a "common concern" for hemispheric defense, although they rejected outright any binding mutual assistance pact.[4]

Hollywood and Washington

Amid this growing national concern, the U.S. film industry rallied to the Roosevelt administration, partly out of patriotism but also because of the nervous-but-necessary marriage that existed between the government and the studios. Furthermore, the

3. Dallek, *American Foreign Policy*, pp. 17–18, 38–39, 62, 65–66, 81; E. David Cronon, "Interpreting the Good Neighbor Policy," *Hispanic American Historical Review*, November 1959, pp. 560–61, 565.

4. Dallek, *American Foreign Policy*, pp. 122–28, 175–78.

shrinkage of outlets for movies in Europe had increased dependence on the Latin American market.[5] The Nazi treatment of Jews also incensed Jewish film producers, like the Warner brothers, who made *Juárez*. All of these factors heavily influenced the making and content of the picture, as did the realities of Hollywood itself in the mid-to-late 1930s.

The decade lies within the industry's so-called Golden Age. Most major studios, like Warners, had survived the Depression in remarkable health, and eighty million Americans still went to the movies each week.[6] But beneath their cape of some successful motion pictures, the movie moguls trembled. Increasing Axis domination of the crucial European market diminished foreign profits so vital to the industry. Furthermore, craft unionization in Hollywood caused strife and disrupted production.[7] The federal government was pursuing an antitrust suit that threatened to divest production companies of their lucrative theater holdings, and the House Committee on Un-American Activities, then headed by Martin Dies of Texas, had begun to rant about supposed Communist infiltration of the industry, which made any political motion picture a potential liability. Warner Brothers headed the producers' movement to defuse the Dies movement, and the congressman later claimed that Warners offered either to make him vice-president of the country or to produce any sort of pro-American movie that Dies recommended. The congressman alleged he did not want to be vice-president, but he did begin to plan with studio assistance a one-million-dollar

5. For loss of European markets by U.S. cinema industry see: Leo C. Rosten, *Hollywood: The Movie Colony; The Movie Makers* (New York: Harcourt, Brace, 1941), p. 160; Garth Jowett, *Film: The Democratic Art* (Boston: Little, Brown, 1976), p. 283; Taylor M. Mills, "History of the Overseas Motion Picture Bureau's Early Operations," 1945, pp. 1–2, Record Group 208, National Archives, Washington, D.C.; *New Masses*, April 11, 1939, p. 28; Kurt Pinthus, "History Directs the Movies," *American Scholar*, October 1941, pp. 484–85, 495; Walter Selden, "Movies and Propaganda," *Forum*, April 1940, p. 212.

6. Selden, "Movies and Propaganda," p. 209; Pinthus, "History Directs," p. 484.

7. Rosten, *Hollywood*, pp. 158–59; Jowett, *Democratic Art*, p. 296; *New Masses*, April 11, 1939, p. 28; "TRA Interviews Lester Cole," *Toward Revolutionary Art* (1975), pp. 4–6; telephone interview with Lester Cole, June 25, 1976.

anti-Communist picture.[8] World War II ended the project and temporarily put the House committee out of business, but Dies himself never gave up. He suggested in 1940 that "communist influence was responsible for subtle but very effective propaganda which appeared in such motion pictures as *Juárez*."[9]

Hollywood avoided pictures with overt political themes in the 1930s, and the industry's own censorship office, headed by the "movie czar" Will Hays, enforced the policy of making pictures for entertainment, not propaganda. Militant and broadly influential censorship groups, such as the Catholic Legion of Decency and the American Legion, threatened to throw up pickets around theaters if film content did not meet their political and social tastes. A number of states and municipalities exercised free-wheeling censorship that made life miserable for screenwriters and producers alike. But the industry could not quarantine itself against world events; motion picture personnel, some of them active leftists, founded the Anti-Nazi League in 1936. Although Jewish producers like the Warners sympathized with the League's condemnation of Nazi anti-Semitism, they despised the organization's flamboyance because it attracted political attention to the industry and invited opportunists like Dies to investigate the movie world. In short, Hollywood was frightened, and the troubled atmosphere underlined its necessity to be all things to all people and to entertain everyone and to offend no one.[10]

8. Jowett, *Democratic Art*, p. 277; U.S., Congress, House, Committee on Un-American Activities, *Investigation of Un-American Propaganda Activities in the United States on H. Res. 282*, 75th Cong., 3d sess., 1938; William Gellermann, *Martin Dies* (New York: Da Capo, 1972), pp. 95ff.; Rosten, *Hollywood*, p. 144; Martin Dies, "More Snakes Than I Can Kill," *Liberty*, February 10, 1940, pp. 42–46; Dies, "The Reds in Hollywood," *Liberty*, February 17, 1940, pp. 47–50; Dies, "Is Communism Invading the Movies?" *Liberty*, February 24, 1940, pp. 57–60; Dies, "No More Immigrants," *Liberty*, March 30, 1940, pp. 12–14.

9. Dies, "Reds in Hollywood," pp. 47–50.

10. *New York Times*, January 15, 1939, sec. 9, p. 5; *New York World Telegram*, June 8, 1939, p. 17, and July 9, 1939, p. 21; Margaret Farrand Thorp, *America at the Movies* (New Haven: Yale University Press, 1940), pp. 214, 273; "Censorship of Motion Pictures," *Yale Law Review Journal*, November 1939, pp. 91–102, 106–107; Jowett, *Democratic Art*, pp. 281, 294; Walter Wanger, "120,000 American

To better its relationship with the government, and with an eye toward financial gain, the film industry had also tried to prove itself a "good neighbor" to Latin Americans. Despite occasional official complaints that a particular film had offended a nation's sensibilities, Latin audiences continued to pay to see Hollywood's often derogatory stereotypes of themselves. The movie *Girl of the Rio* (1932), however, had so outraged Mexican feelings that it became part of the agenda at the 1936 Inter-American Conference in Buenos Aires. The unflattering portrayal of their ordinary countrymen had not much offended Mexican officials, but the portrayal of the country's upper crust as lecherous and greedy certainly did. Discussions in a conference subcommittee led to an agreement that pictures that distorted history or insulted the traditions of any one country would not be distributed to any of the member nations.[11]

Hollywood further tried to help Roosevelt strengthen hemi-

Ambassadors," *Foreign Affairs*, October 1939, p. 46; Meyer Levin, "The Candid Cameraman: Hollywood Producers Submit to Dictators Incidentally Giving America War-Minded Films," *Esquire*, November 1936, p. 125; "Film Censorship: An Administrative Analysis," *Columbia Law Review*, December 1939, pp. 1384–1402; [Will H. Hays], *The Memoirs of Will H. Hays* (Garden City, N.Y.: Doubleday, 1955), p. 142; Richard Corliss, "The Legion of Decency," *Film Comment*, Summer 1968, pp. 24–61; Richard S. Randall, *Censorship of the Movies: The Social and Political Control of a Mass Medium* (Madison: University of Wisconsin Press, 1970), pp. 28–29, 129, 161–162, 199–200; Charles A. Beard and Mary R. Beard, *America in Midpassage* (New York: Macmillan, 1939), p. 601; Ben Ray Redman, "Pictures and Censorship," *Saturday Review of Literature*, December 3, 1938, p. 13.

11. Cordell Hull, *The Memoirs of Cordell Hull*, vol. 1 (New York: Macmillan, 1948), p. 493; *Inter-American Conference for the Maintenance of Peace: Proceedings*, stenographic reports (Buenos Aires: Imprenta del Congreso Nacional, 1937), p. 532; U.S., Department of State, Record Group 59, Decimal File 811.4061, Motion Pictures/259, Box 5204, National Archives, Washington, D.C. (hereafter cited as SD); Allen Woll, *The Latin Image in American Film* (Los Angeles: UCLA Latin American Center Publications, University of California, 1977). For *Girl of the Río* see: Woll, *Latin Image*, pp. 21, 33, 37, 49; *New York Times*, January 9, 1932, p. 21, and April 20, 1932, p. 27; George H. Roeder, Jr., "Mexicans in the Movies: The Image of Mexicans in American Films, 1894–1947," paper (University of Wisconsin, 1971), bibliographical section, p. 28; DeWitt Bodeen, "Dolores del Río," *Films in Review*, May 1967, pp. 271, 278–79.

spheric commitments among the American nations at the Inter-American Conference of 1938. Will Hays wrote to Roosevelt on November 18, 1938, that the Motion Picture Producers Association would provide full motion picture coverage of the conference. After the meeting, the producers offered to send a camera crew throughout Latin America to photograph sequences that could then be spliced into future newsreels. Hays ironed out details with the State Department and informed the president that his employees would photograph "such news as may be believed by the State Department to be of special value." Hollywood would, of course, pay the bill, and in discussing other aspects of the administration's film program for Latin America, Hays assured FDR that the film producers "all are enthusiastic to co-operate in every possible way."[12]

"Cooperation" between the federal government and the industry also meant scrapping motion pictures that Washington sensed did not serve the national interests. When the administration learned in early 1939 that Metro-Goldwyn Mayer intended to dramatize the crash of the Imperial Airways flying boat *Cavalier,* which had gone down on its recent New York City–Bermuda flight, the State Department intervened. That very week Eleanor Roosevelt was to christen a Pan-American seventy-four-passenger clipper to inaugurate a transatlantic flight service that the government had heavily subsidized. G. S. Messersmith of the State Department on March 1 hurried a note to Will Hays: "Keeping in mind that our government and our people have a very definite interest in the success of such trans-Atlantic flights, I believe that you will agree that it would be much more appropriate to dramatize the first successful flight by an American airliner rather than revive an already dead incident."[13] Hays agreed and so informed MGM, which dropped plans for the picture.[14]

12. Hays to Roosevelt, November 18, 1938, Franklin Delano Roosevelt Personal Papers, File 1945, Franklin Delano Roosevelt Library, Hyde Park, N.Y. (hereafter cited as FDR MSS).

13. Thomas Burke to G. S. Messersmith, February 27, 1939, SD, 811.4061, Motion Pictures/259, and George S. Messersmith to Will Hays, March 1, 1939.

14. SD, 811.4061, Motion Pictures/26-263.

FDR and Jack Warner

The continual exchange between Hollywood and Washington was most often conducted at this high level, but none was higher than the communication between the Warner brothers and Franklin Roosevelt. Jack Warner, head of the company's productions, had in 1932 successfully managed Roosevelt's presidential campaign in California, starting a comradeship that lasted until the president's death. "It was no secret on the lot," Warner wrote in his autobiography, "that I admired Franklin Delano Roosevelt, that I had a personal friendship with him any man would envy, and that I had been his guest many times at the White House."[15] The tone of their correspondence does indeed indicate that they were at least personal acquaintances. They even traveled the Potomac together on the presidential yacht.[16] One film scholar states that the president frequently served as technical adviser on Warner's political films, while Hal Wallis, the producer who in the late 1930s was directly in charge of major Warner Brothers pictures, still remembers Eleanor Roosevelt's frequent presence on the sets at the company's Burbank, California, studio.[17]

The Roosevelt–Warner Brothers connection naturally yielded mutual benefits. When the Hollywood Rider Actors Association complained to the government in 1937 that its members had been deprived of work because the studio had been granted army men and materiel to make *Sergeant Murphy* at the Presidio in Monterey, California, Jack Warner informed the president that the picture, which portrayed the army in a favorable light, could not be made without army cooperation. One of Roosevelt's secretaries took up the matter with the War Depart-

15. Jack L. Warner with Dean Jennings, *My First Hundred Years in Hollywood* (New York: Random House, 1964), p. 285.

16. For examples see: Jack Warner to Marvin H. McIntyre, July 8, 1937, FDR MSS, File 73, Motion Pictures, July–October 1937; Warner to McIntyre, December 23, 1938, November–December 1938; Warner to Roosevelt, April 28, 1939, January–April, 1939.

17. Ina Rae Hark, "The Visual Politics of 'Adventures of Robin Hood,'" *Journal of Popular Film* (1976), p. 6; interview with Hal Wallis, Los Angeles, August 11, 1976.

ment and the president's military aide, and Warner received permission to use government men and equipment for a movie expected to be so "educational and helpful."[18] Jack Warner thanked the president. "It's just things like this that make a fellow feel real good when he has a just and right cause."[19]

Harry Warner, the financial genius of the company, wrote confidentially to Roosevelt on September 5, 1939, that he had just returned to New York from Great Britain where blackouts, air raid precautions, and the removal of urban population to rural districts had all but emptied motion picture houses in England's big cities. With France falling into Nazi hands, "we will have to operate at a loss. For how long, who knows?" Warner further explained that with Hollywood besieged by federal litigation (of which the antitrust suit was the most worrisome part), preparations for the legal defense of such cases had further drained the company of time, manpower, and money. "If we are to work out of the difficulties imposed by the European war, [we] must be freed of [the] burden of litigation. Two hundred and forty thousand employees of the Industry and hundreds of thousands of stockholders desire to avoid bankruptcy."[20]

Warner's observations found the desk of Harry Hopkins, secretary of commerce. The antitrust case ended in a consent agreement on November 14, 1940, and the government pressed the issue no more at that time.[21]

As payment for Jack Warner's campaign services in California, Roosevelt had in 1932 offered him a diplomatic post. Warner declined, saying he was flattered, "but I think I can do better for your foreign relations with a good picture about America now and then."[22] *Juárez* was, in part then, a fulfillment of that com-

18. Jack Warner to McIntyre, July 8–9, 1937, FDR MSS, File 73, Motion Pictures, July–October 1937.

19. Warner to McIntyre, July 10, 1937, FDR MSS, File 73, Motion Pictures, July–October 1937.

20. Harry Warner to Roosevelt, September 5, 1939, FDR MSS, File 73, Motion Pictures, September–December 1939.

21. S. T. Early to General Edwin Watson, September 6, 1939, FDR MSS, File 73, Motion Pictures, September–December 1939; Jowett, *Democratic Art*, 277–78.

22. Warner, *My First Hundred Years*, p. 224.

mitment, but the movie also responded to other needs and designs of the Warner brothers: the company's representative in Germany, a Jew, had been brutally bludgeoned to death in 1935 by Nazi thugs, and his death begged for revenge. The Dies committee had launched a hunt for un-Americanism in Hollywood, and the picture would confirm the studio's patriotism. Besides, its historical biography series, which featured *The Life of Emile Zola* and *The Life of Louis Pasteur,* had been a critical and financial success and merited a successor, and its most popular and highly paid actor, Paul Muni, needed a new role. With all this in mind, Warner Brothers decided to make *Juárez* its greatest production ever. The budget was set at $1.75 million, highest in the company's history. The picture would be photographed with a new, fast film, which would enhance the black and gray tones and permit a textured, three-dimensional effect. Mexico City was to be re-created on the company's eleven-acre ranch in Calabasas, and there would be no hurry. The writers had a year or more to develop the script. Warners was extremely proud of its recent "serious historical work," but Jack Warner assured the industry and the public, "You ain't seen nothin' yet!"[23]

In the late 1930s, as Americans searched for an explanation of the Depression and a blueprint for the next decades, they frequently focused upon the nation's past, where they discovered heroes, a folklore, and other strengths that augured well for the country.[24] A new nationalism spread, fueled, in part, by economic interests. As summarized by Alfred Kazin, the movement "began by reporting the ravages of the depression and ended by reporting on the national inheritance."[25] Historical studies, especially scholarly biographies, abounded as writers burrowed backward into the national consciousness to discover how their predecessors had survived the pressures of their most

23. Hark, "Visual Politics," p. 4; interview with Henry Blanke, Los Angeles, August 10, 1976; Jerome Lawrence, *Actor: The Life and Times of Paul Muni* (New York: Putnam, 1974), pp. 235, 241–42.

24. Alfred Haworth Jones, *Roosevelt's Image Brokers: Poets, Playwrights, and the Use of the Lincoln Symbol* (Port Washington, N.Y.: Kennikat, 1974), pp. 13–14.

25. Alfred Kazin, *On Native Grounds* (New York: Harcourt, Brace and World, 1942), p. 487.

difficult times. Research dug up "facts"—the authors hung the data together in elaborate detail. The nationalism that coated this outpouring was isolationist in tone; it stressed American ideals and values, such as democracy, and largely, it turned its back on Europe.[26]

The studio had by then already curried government favor with its picture *The Monroe Doctrine*, intended for distribution in Latin America. Before release, the movie was submitted to the State Department for comment, and Adolf A. Berle, Jr., assistant secretary of state for Latin American affairs, recommended that several scenes be deleted, especially a speech by President Theodore Roosevelt, because "the speech in question was followed by the beginning of intervention in the Dominican Republic—an intervention which obliterated the Dominican government for nearly ten years and embittered Latin America until it [the intervention] was liquidated."[27] In making *Juárez*, the studio faced the same problem: how to criticize intervention in Latin America by French imperialists and yet not remind the "good neighbors" about intervention by North American democrats.

It was in this atmosphere that one of the Warner Brothers studio's highly regarded screenwriters, Aeneas MacKenzie, began to amass data and to outline the contours of events that would, in a motion picture, match the democrat Juárez against the imperialist Maximilian, would bind Mexico's fortunes more closely to the United States than history had done, and would establish parallels between the nineteenth-century French interventionists and Europe's contemporary dictators. The movie was to stress the successful resistance of the hemisphere (actually Mexico) to past European intervention (supposedly due to the Monroe Doctrine) and was to urge new solidarity—under United States leadership—against the new threat. From the beginning the orders to the screenwriter were clear: "The dialogue, as far as it is political and ideological, must consist of

26. Kazin, *On Native Grounds*, p. 505; Jones, *Image Brokers*, pp. 12–19.

27. Adolf A. Berle, Jr., to Joseph Hazen, October 7, 1939, SD, 811.4061, *Monroe Doctrine* THE/2.

phrases from today's newspapers; every child must be able to recognize that Napoleon in his Mexican intervention is none other than Mussolini plus Hitler in their Spanish adventure."[28]

MacKenzie's research was worthy of a professional historian. He assembled more than seven hundred books and another two thousand letters, diaries, and documents—some in Spanish, others in French—as source materials for his project, and he enlisted the aid of a New York University professor, Jesse John Dossick, to develop an overview of those tumultuous few years of Mexico's past, 1861–67.[29]

Mexico's Ordeal

Following three centuries of Spanish colonial rule, Mexico won independence in the 1820s and emerged as a republic, confirmed by its Constitution of 1824. For the next fifty years domestic factions fought over the right to direct the nation's fortunes, internecine strife that cost the country half of its patrimony to the United States. One group of conservatives believed royal authority was needed to restore order and searched Europe for a candidate as king. Meanwhile, liberal republicans promoted land and other reforms that attacked privileges long held by the conservative elite. After three years of especially bitter civil war, the liberals under President Benito Juárez in 1861 won a tenuous hold on the capital and nominal charge of the nation's affairs. Because their treasury had been emptied by war, the Juárez government could not pay off a debt owed to France, which gave that nation's emperor, Louis Napoleon, a pretext to pursue in Mexico his imperialist bent. Times for such adventures were especially opportune; the United States, which most assuredly would have questioned such intervention as a

28. Wolfgang Reinhardt, "Phantom Crown," February 15, 1938, Document 8, Box 5, William Dieterle Collection 17, Doheny Library, University of Southern California, Los Angeles (hereafter cited as Dieterle Collection).

29. Many of the original research materials are at the Library of the Academy of Motion Picture Arts and Sciences, Beverly Hills, Calif. (Boxes 5 and 6, Dieterle Collection 17, *Juárez*); Paul Muni Collection, Theater Collection of the Library and Museum of the Performing Arts, Lincoln Center, New York City Library (hereafter cited as Muni Collection).

violation of the Monroe Doctrine, was embroiled in its own civil war. The Mexican monarchists, abetted by Napoleon, devised a fraudulent plebiscite to convince the Austrian archduke, Maximilian von Hapsburg, that masses of Mexicans approved him as their emperor, and Louis promised military support until Maximilian was firmly seated on his new throne. Mexican republicans vigorously resisted the intrusion upon their sovereignty, but by 1864 French troops had cleared a path to the capital to permit the arrival of Maximilian and his Belgian wife, Carlotta.

From the start events went badly for the monarchists. Not only did republican guerrilla activity persist, but Maximilian himself seemed more in tune with the *Juaristas* than with the people who had brought him to Mexico. He alienated conservatives by refusing to rescind many of the liberal reform measures earlier dictated by the Juárez government. The Catholic church, for instance, did not regain the land that the Liberals had nationalized. Maximilian believed property should be more equally divided than in the past, and he decreed that common Mexicans should continue to enjoy many of the rights accorded them under the republican Constitution of 1857. Maximilian, unable to have children by Carlotta, solved the delicate succession question by adopting a Mexican son and naming him archduke. Yet, resistance to his presence continued: Juárez had competent generals and perhaps fifteen thousand men in the north, and Colonel Porfirio Díaz had his quick-striking guerrilla forces south of the capital. A distraught Maximilian finally decreed harsh penalties, even death, for Mexicans who aided the republicans, a desperate act that contradicted his former leniency.

With Mexican monarchist support dwindling and the imperial treasury empty, the royalists' days were numbered, and the end of the American Civil War plus Napoleon's decision to return his army to France finished the enterprise. Carlotta reminded Napoleon of his promises and sought assistance from Europe's royalty to no avail. Maximilian could have left Mexico with the departing French troops but chose to stay to defend his royalist commitment, a decision that led to his execution in June 1867, despite worldwide pleas for clemency.[30] Mexico's republicans had defeated the European imperialists, no doubt about that, but in 1938 Aeneas MacKenzie had to mold that historic occurrence into an urgent and effective call for cooperative hemispheric defense.

The Screenwriters' Predicament

In the distillation of the historical material into production notes, which he began on September 30, 1937, MacKenzie became fascinated with and somewhat mystical about the ordinary Zapotec Indian who had somehow become president of Mexico and expelled European royalty from his native land. He described Juárez as having a "heavy head set deeply into rugged shoulders [that] suggests *Pithecanthropus*—an emergence of mentality from matter [see figure 5]. A modern artist would probably model him to convey the impression of a solid mass, struggling a way out of rock, capable of inflexible movement only as an entity and in a straight line." MacKenzie also explained how Indians move: "Indians do not look about them and Indians do not talk to one another as they go along the road to their destination. Benito Pablo Juárez at heart was at all times a Zapotec Indian."[31] With remarkable candor, not to speak of racial misunderstanding, MacKenzie saw Juárez as disadvantaged in his struggle for public support to combat the interlopers. The dark-skinned Zapotec "had to contend . . . with the dazzling figure of a Hapsburg emperor, whose great golden beard suggested a

30. Best work in English on Juárez is Ralph Roeder's *Juárez and His Mexico*, 2 vols. (New York: Greenwood Press, 1968). Jack Autrey Dabbs emphasizes military aspects of the intervention in *The French Army in Mexico, 1861–1867: A Study in Military Government* (The Hague: Mouton, 1963). An older but still useful volume on the intervention from a European point of view is Percy F. Martin's *Maximilian in Mexico: The Story of the French Intervention* (New York: Scribner's, 1914).

31. "The Character and Career of Benito Juárez," September 10, 1937, p. 1, *Juárez*, Warner Film Library, Wisconsin Center for Film and Theater Research, Madison, Wis. (hereafter cited as Warner library). A "Pithecanthropus" is an extinct ape, if the animal ever existed, that had a very low forehead, underdeveloped chin, the posture of a modern man, but a brain smaller than that of modern man.

reincarnation of the Fair God *Quetzalcoatl*. And beside Maximilian stood the beauteous Empress of the Shining Eyes, before which a hating, subject race had already bowed down in adoration. Against such glamorous figures, how could a poor ape-like Indian hope to survive in the hearts of people which scorned his humble and downtrodden breed?"[32] Hidebound by his concept of beauty, MacKenzie never understood that Quetzalcoatl was a Toltec Indian, not some Nordic god, and that virtually all Mexicans were either Indian or mestizo. The writer also found Juárez obtuse: "It was typical of the Indian that he did not foresee the obvious factor that was to make for his complete and final victory. Never for an instant did Juárez credit the possible intervention of the United States on his behalf" (figure 17). Finally, he concluded that "Juárez was never a genius; he never exhibited resource or cleverness, but kept in his path in blind faith and a willingness to endure."[33] MacKenzie obviously had some respect for Benito Juárez, but his preconceptions and prejudices favored the royal couple, sentiments that he wrote, perhaps unintentionally, into the screenplay and which eventually affected the picture.

What intrigued MacKenzie most about Juárez was the Indian's escape from Catholic socialization to become a zealot for freedom. Juárez had gone to a Catholic seminary, wrote MacKenzie, where he "commenced to discover how many angels could dance on the point of a needle, and just what God on his cloud did when it began to rain. For six years he pursued the theological mysteries, and submitted to the humiliating discipline of the seminary."[34] Actually, Juárez had never become steeped in church lore, and early on as a law student and politician he followed liberal aims, which were intensely anticlerical but not necessarily anti-Catholic. But MacKenzie did not need to

32. MacKenzie, "The Character and Career of Benito Juárez," p. 18; MacKenzie, "The Patriots," p. 3, Production Materials Number 59, studio production materials archive, Warner Brothers Studios, Burbank, California (hereafter cited as Warner Brothers Studios).

33. MacKenzie, "The Character and Career of Benito Juárez," pp. 4, 17–18.

34. A. E. MacKenzie, "Historical Period of Benito Pablo Juárez," August 26, 1937, p. 5, Warner library.

trouble himself with the church; the church was not to be at issue in this picture, even though it might have been important in Mexican history. In fact, the picture studiously avoids mention of Catholic matters. It reworks the property issue by having Juárez confiscate the lands of the hacendados, rather than the church. It simply would not have been timely in 1938 for Hollywood to raise any Catholic issue—especially with regard to Mexico. For a decade or more Mexico's government had literally been at war with the church; it took Catholic property, limited its role in education, expelled its priests, restricted its politics, hushed its voice. U.S. Catholics continued to raise a furor over the Mexican crusade against the church and to demand official U.S. sanctions against "godless" Mexico. At the same time, but for opposite reasons, Mexican censors were also sensitive to pictures that concerned church and state.[35] So a movie calculated to induce hemispheric cooperation simply had to skirt the Catholic issue, even if it meant the rearrangement of history. Many similar considerations robbed the movie of historical accuracy but paradoxically make it a more valuable contemporary historical document.

To avoid potential copyright difficulties with its movie, Warner Brothers secured film rights to a play and a historical novel loosely based on the story of the intervention. Franz Werfel's 1926 play, *Juárez and Maximilian*, did provide the dramatic structure for the picture, even if the play had arrived at the opposite political conclusion. In Werfel's climactic scene, Maximilian admits, "My idea of a radical monarchy was unreal. . . . The age of royalty is over. In the shipwreck of the privileged classes poor little kings who are not kings must perish. The hour of *dictators* [my emphasis] has come. Juárez [is here]."[36] So Juárez, a dictator in 1926, had to be recast as a democrat in 1938.

35. E. David Cronon, *Josephus Daniels in Mexico* (Madison: University of Wisconsin Press, 1960), pp. 84–85; Dallek, *American Foreign Policy*, pp. 123–24; Eugene Harley, *World-Wide Influence of Cinema: A Study of Official Censorship and the International Cultural Aspects of Motion Pictures* (Los Angeles: University of Southern California Press, 1940), p. 167.

36. Franz Werfel, *Juárez and Maximilian: A Dramatic History in Three Phases and Thirteen Pictures*, trans. Ruth Langner (New York: Simon & Schuster, 1926), p. 146.

Such conversions provided no problems for the screenwriter, but the characterizations of Maximilian and Carlotta did. The ill-fated adventure of the well-intentioned couple is the sort of romantic drama of which movies are made, and the filmmakers never managed to divert audience appeal from the star-struck royalists to the emotionless, dark-skinned Juárez. It seemed to studio heads reading the script that Maximilian had beaten Juárez—the totalitarians had won out over the democrats—or at least that is the way audiences would understand it. The studio assigned other writers to the project to assist MacKenzie in addressing these difficulties: the meticulous Wolfgang Reinhart, an energetically rambunctious, thirty-two-year-old John Huston, and dialogue specialist Abem Finkel. But even the rather desperate final editing of the movie, in which the filmmakers excised some of the sequences that featured the gentle, well-bred Maximilian (Brian Aherne) and his devoted, clever wife, Carlotta (Bette Davis), failed to resolve the problem. The benign images were imbedded in the picture (figures 6, 7, 8, 12, 22). The writers understood all along that they were to "consider the screen as a campaign platform. Will the audience vote for monarchy or democracy?" But they never could resolve the continuing concerns of studio viewers: "We, the audience, are beginning to think that Maximilian may be right. Monarchy sounds pretty good."[37]

Teaching Democracy

New drafts of the script became steadily more didactic. The writers meant to teach the difference between democracy and totalitarianism. Once again they bent history. In meetings that never occurred, except in the movie, Maximilian convinces Porfirio Díaz (John Garfield), who had been captured by the monarchists, of the emperor's liberal intentions toward Mexico.

MAXIMILIAN: What is it that he [Juárez] wants?

37. "General Notes on *Phantom Crown*, 1938," p. 59, and "Consolidation of the Values of Scenes 10 and 13," *Juárez*, Warner Brothers Studios; Whitney Stine, *Mother Goddam: The Story of the Career of Bette Davis* (New York: Hawthorn, 1974), p. 114; Lawrence, *Paul Muni*, pp. 241–42; William F. Nolan, *John Huston: King Rebel* (Los Angeles: Sherbourne Press, 1965), pp. 37–38.

DÍAZ: To put an end to the things that he himself has endured. To educate, to liberate, to uplift through democracy.

MAXIMILIAN: Then all that lies between us is a word, General Díaz, for otherwise Benito Juárez and I are in accord.

The word, of course, is *democracy*. Maximilian agrees that in theory democracy is an ideal system, but that it does not work because "government by the people can become the rule of a mob." Also, "a president is a politician and must answer to his party. But a king is above factions and parties. A president may be poor and therefore open to temptation, but a king, having everything, desires nothing."

Díaz is released from jail to carry the good news to Juárez; the monarch wants Juárez to be his prime minister. In response, Juárez becomes more solemn than ever:

JUÁREZ: Maximiliano says only a word stands between him and me. Only the word *democracy*. Porfirio, what does it mean, this word?

DÍAZ: Democracy? (Laughing.) Why, it means liberty—liberty for a man to say what he thinks. To worship as he believes. It means equal opportunity.

JUÁREZ: No. No, that cannot be its meaning, Porfirio. Maximiliano offers us all these things without democracy. What is it then that he would withhold from us?

DÍAZ: Er, only the right to rule ourselves.

JUÁREZ: Then that must be the meaning of the word, Porfirio. . . . The right of every man to rule himself and the nation in which he lives. And since no man rules himself into bondage, therefore liberty flows from it as water from the hills. . . .

Only a word, *democracy*, may stand between Maximiliano von Hapsburg and myself, but it is an unbridgeable gulf. We represent irreconcilable principles, one or the other of which must perish. You see, Porfirio, when a monarch misrules, he changes the people; when a presidente misrules, the people change him [figure 13].

Díaz assured his president that he now understood—but the producers continued to worry that the audiences would not do the same:

On one hand we have Maximilian developing a fairly practical case for benevolent monarchy. His benevolence seems to outweigh the tenacity of Juárez who talks about his zeal for theoretical democracy. On the other hand we have a factual demonstration of both forms of government existing today. England is a benevolent monarchy and America is a flourishing democracy. Consider the impact of the Maximilian and Juárez contentions on our audience. The script accentuates the virtues of monarchy.[38]

When the picture was released, spectators reacted as the producers had feared. They seemed more sympathetic to monarchy, although not necessarily Great Britain.

English sensibilities further complicated matters for the screenwriters, along with the knowledge that many Americans deeply felt their common heritage with Great Britain. But in 1938 U.S. public opinion was not entirely disposed toward British pacifism; many believed that Hitler and Mussolini had backed down the English with bombast.[39] Roosevelt himself was stressing hemispheric solidarity as opposed to a British alliance; therefore, the filmmakers eliminated only the most potentially inflammatory statements concerning the British and hoped that moviegoers understood that European imperialism meant contemporary fascism and not constitutional monarchy. Near the end of the final screenplay, when European diplomats request an audience with Juárez to plead for Maximilian's life, the officially dressed British ambassador had advised his German counterpart: "Ah, my dear Baron, you Germans are inexperienced in the handling of native races. A bit of gold braid goes the deuce of a long way with these Mexican Johnnies" (scene 272). That statement was edited out of the final cut. But the British emissary remains present in the scene where Juárez reads out the diplomats in what was meant to be the most telling point of the movie:

By what right, señores, do the great powers of Europe invade the lands of simple people, kill all who do not make them welcome, destroy their fields and take the fruit of their toil from those who survive? Is it a crime against God, then, that the skin of some men is of a different

38. "General Notes on *Phantom Crown*, 1938," p. 59.

39. William E. Leuchtenburg, *Franklin D. Roosevelt and the New Deal, 1932–1940* (New York: Harper & Row, 1963), p. 288.

> color? That they do not wear shoes upon their feet? They know nothing of factories and commerce?
>
> The world must know that one generous in purpose [Maximilian] was duped to his death by the vanity of power-drunk dictators! . . . The world must know the fate of any foreign usurper who sets his foot upon this soil. . . . The world must know that Mexico is not a spoil for the butchering, exploiting powers of your European civilization.

When world events moved more quickly than the picture, Juárez further sharpened his position. In the script of June 2, 1938, Díaz makes one final appeal for the monarch's life. "Don Benito, you cannot let him die," and then, gazing at the portrait of Abraham Lincoln that Juárez kept close by (in the film), Díaz wondered,

> What would he do, Don Benito? Democracy is a human thing . . . It is warm and living because it is of the people themselves . . . It is not cold, relentless justice . . .
>
> JUÁREZ (rising from his chair, and in a tone which is almost a cry of pain): Do I not know . . . ? Do you think I want him to die?

Munich—September 29, 1938—eliminated that exchange. The Munich agreement meant more conquest by negotiation for Adolph Hitler. Czechoslovakia, a democracy, was sold out. Before these events democracy may have been a "human thing," but after Munich, no more compromises, at least not for Warner Brothers. Moreover, the Good Neighbor Policy required new cement. The Mexican government had, the previous March, expropriated foreign oil holdings, among them substantial U.S. interests, and American businesspeople urged revenge, even while Roosevelt counseled patience.[40]

The Resurrection of Lincoln

Abraham Lincoln, meanwhile, stayed right in place. In their endeavor to chain the fortunes of Mexico to the United States and the rest of the hemisphere, the screenwriters relied on Lincoln. The Great Emancipator was an excellent choice. In their

40. Dallek, *American Foreign Policy*, pp. 166, 171, 173, 175–76; Cronon, *Josephus Daniels*, pp. 127, 223–36.

search for historical precedents to prove the soundness of their republic, Americans had focused upon Lincoln.

Lincoln ensured the future for Depression era Americans—not all, but most. He had once before saved the Union and liberated the slaves, and now, in the 1930s, he encouraged people to scramble from beneath the new disaster. Lincoln represented democratic traditions and free institutions, phrases that became public lifelines to the future. "At a time when American democracy has reached a crisis which many think it cannot survive," wrote Bernard DeVoto, "the American people have invoked the man who, by general consent, represents the highest reach of the American character and who, in that earlier crisis, best embodied the strength of our democracy. . . . What America finds in Lincoln is confirmation of the best it has dared to believe of itself. . . . He is the highest expression of American democracy. Of the democracy that survived its test."[41] Kazin found "the passionate addiction to Lincoln" among "the most moving aspects" of the decade.[42] Writers manifested their genuine passion for Lincoln in such masterpiece works as Robert E. Sherwood's play *Abe Lincoln in Illinois* and in *Abraham Lincoln: The War Years,* four brilliant historical volumes by Carl Sandburg. Emanuel Hertz revealed the *Hidden Lincoln,* and Tyler Dennett selected letters and diaries of John Hay to review *Lincoln and the Civil War.* And in the public mentality Lincoln merged with Franklin Delano Roosevelt.[43]

Roosevelt deliberately wrapped himself in Lincoln's cloak, not only for political self-interest but because FDR understood the uses of history as a unifying force in national affairs. Lincoln offered the best in the liberal tradition and democratic ideals; he justified New Deal policies. In the late 1930s the president used Lincoln to support his foreign policy.[44] All this identification rankled ex-President Hoover, who remarked at a Lincoln Day dinner in 1939 that both Roosevelt and a communist boss had

41. Bernard DeVoto, "Father Abraham," *Harper's*, February 1940, pp. 333–36.

42. Alfred Kazin, *New York Herald Tribune Books*, December 31, 1939, p. 1.

43. Jones, *Image Brokers, passim*; *New York World Telegram*, June 10, 1939, p. 4.

44. Jones, *Image Brokers*, pp. 3–4, 64–69; *New York Times*, April 27, 1938, p. 22, and May 1, 1938, sec. 4, p. 8.

claimed Lincoln "as founder of their faiths." Hoover reminded the gathering that Lincoln had been a Republican and concluded, "Whatever this New Deal system is, it is certain that it did not come from Abraham Lincoln."[45]

Roosevelt lived up to the challenge: "I do not know which party Lincoln would belong to if he were alive in 1940—and I am not even concerned to speculate on it; . . . I am more interested in the fact that he did the big job which then had to be done—to preserve the Union and make possible, at a later time, the united country that we all live in today."[46]

The president did not have to draw the parallels between himself and Lincoln. Others did it for him. Sandburg wrote to FDR, "I have my eyes and ears in two eras and cannot help drawing parallels. One runs to the effect that you are the best light of democracy that has occupied the White House since Lincoln."[47] Sherwood invited Roosevelt to his play: "I hope that some day you will honor this play with your presence. I think it shows quite clearly how Lincoln stood on most present issues in our country and abroad."[48] New York's popular and colorful mayor, Fiorello LaGuardia, predicted that "seventy-five years from today our present president, Franklin Delano Roosevelt, will be hailed as a liberator, just as we are hailing Lincoln today."[49] And finally Max Lerner wrote: "How much of Lincoln does Roosevelt have in him? More, I am convinced, than any president since Lincoln or before."[50] Lincoln had unified America; so would FDR. Jack Warner aimed to make that connection in his motion picture—and to expand its dimensions: Lincoln had once saved all the American nations from European imperialism, and, implicitly, Roosevelt would now do the same.

Read those wonderful Warner Brothers press releases on

45. *New York Times*, February 14, 1939, p. 14.

46. *The Public Papers and Addresses of Franklin D. Roosevelt . . . 1940 Volume: War—and Aid to Democracies* (New York: Macmillan, 1941), p. 30.

47. Quoted in Jones, *Image Brokers*, p. 76.

48. Quoted in Jones, *Image Brokers*, p. 42.

49. *New York Times*, February 13, 1940, p. 25.

50. Max Lerner, "Men Who Would Be President: IX. Franklin D. Roosevelt," *Nation*, June 22, 1940, p. 753.

Juárez: "Lincoln was his [Juárez's] hero." "Benito Juárez . . . Poor but proud Indian of old Mexico . . . Fights his way to the presidency of his native land . . . and . . . inspired by the ideals of the Great Emancipator . . . becomes the arch-advocate of the oppressed." A poster in theater lobbies read, "America has two heroes: Lincoln and Thee [Juárez], Lincoln by whom slavery has died and Thee by whom liberty has lived." Actually, Juárez admired Lincoln but never expected substantial assistance from the United States in his struggle against the French. Even following the Civil War, when the United States applied a bit of diplomatic pressure on Louis Napoleon, Juárez wrote: "I have never had illusions with regard to the open aid that that nation [United States] could give us. I know that the rich and the powerful do not feel or try to alleviate the miseries of the poor. The former fear and respect each other and are not able to break lances in the quarrels of the weak or against the injustices with which they are oppressed. This is and has been the way of the world. Only those who do not recognize it deceive themselves."[51]

Historical accuracy, however, does not much concern Hollywood's screenwriters; for them, it is the story that counts. In the case of *Juárez*, they invented a friendship between Lincoln and the Mexican president which for Benito Juárez, the supposedly emotionless Indian, bordered on adoration (figures 3, 9, 13, 21). The various scripts are punctuated with suggestions to make the movie ever more Lincolnlike: the letter that Juárez writes to Maximilian "could be made a model of Lincolnian simplicity," and when Juárez forgives a follower for his misgivings about the republican cause, "omit the political expediency and cold calculation of the gesture and make it a movement of Lincolnian magnanimity."[52]

No one tried harder than Paul Muni as Juárez to pack more of Lincoln into the picture. "Try to get in the connection between Lincoln and Juárez," he told the writers, "not only that he

51. Charles Allen Smart, *Viva Juárez!: A Biography* (Philadelphia: Lippincott, 1963), p. 355.

52. "Juárez the Impossible," Document 8, Box 5, Dieterle Collection 17.

[Juárez] has a picture of him [Lincoln] in the room, but that they corresponded with each other. Not that Juárez was an admirer from afar, but that they had actual contact [figure 3]."[53] In the movie *Bordertown* (1935) Muni had played the role of a Mexican-American who became a lawyer and whose ideal was Lincoln, so Muni was familiar with Lincoln-inspired individuals, but he claimed that he knew nothing of Benito Juárez until he traveled for six weeks in Mexico in the preproduction phase of *Juárez*. The reason for the dearth of information on Juárez seemed obvious to Muni. The Mexican was a contemporary of Lincoln, and the U.S. Civil War had overshadowed the Mexican intervention. "Plus, Mexico itself had no great historians." But on the tour of Mexico, according to the press book, Muni discovered Juárez to be "much like Lincoln, a man born in abject poverty, absolutely self-educated, who rose by the brilliant powers of his own mind to save the nation who had born him. Juárez not only rekindled the great flame of democracy in Mexico, but he kept it alive during the time the powers of Europe established a dictator monarch, Maximilian, on its throne."

Mexico's President Lázaro Cárdenas had invited Muni to Mexico in September 1938 as a goodwill gesture toward the famous actor, and because Cárdenas needed to do some fence mending of his own. The oil expropriation issue still boiled, and his government needed loans and investment capital from the United States. The movie's director, William Dieterle, and producers Wallis and Blanke went along to survey the historical setting of their picture and to learn more particulars about Juárez the man. They reported interviews with several elderly *Juaristas*—one of them 116 years old—about the president's lifestyle, and Muni emerged convinced that Juárez had "changed the course of history of both Europe and the Americas." He also noted that "the parallel between the attempt of a 19th century Paris-London-Vienna axis seeking to reduce Mexico to a protectorate and a field for exploitation and what is going on in the

53. Document 2, Box 5, Dieterle Collection 17; Roeder, "Mexicans in the Movies," bibliographical section, p. 29.

world today is too close to be ignored," and impending war in Europe did create a new urgency for the project.[54]

The Director's Omens

William Dieterle, a tall, dark-eyed, somewhat stiff, ex-German filmmaker, was among the most meticulous and disciplined of Hollywood's directors. He followed the script—period. Dieterle wore white gloves to work in case he had to touch an actor's face to improve a camera angle, and in the prisoner sequence of *Juárez*, when John Garfield as Díaz had to eat corn and speak at the same time, the director insisted that the food be Mexican corn. It was nearing winter and the only Mexican corn available was at a University of California experimental agricultural station. Dieterle ordered it anyway, at four dollars an ear, plus handling, and Garfield ate a good many dollars worth of Mexican corn during the three days that it took to shoot the scene (figure 11).[55]

Besides being such a stickler for detail, Dieterle believed that success and fortune lay in numbers and the stars. The rhythms of numerology and astrology guided his work. Although he set initial shooting on *Juárez* for November 15, the celestial signs for that evening seemed not right, so Dieterle made an insert shot of a poster being ripped from a wall (figure 2) on October 29, when celestial signs were more promising. He took a similar bow to numerology. As the title *Juárez* contained six letters, Dieterle hesitated to use the traditional, "Lights, camera, action"—all words with six letters—to start the cameras. Instead he shouted, "Here—we—go," words with more propitious numbers of letters.[56]

In the movie, as in real life, Juárez and Maximilian never meet. Dieterle first made all of the scenes involving Maximilian

54. Stine, *Mother Goddam*, pp. 114–15; Lawrence, *Paul Muni*, pp. 241–42; Bruce Pinter, "Another Biography Is Added to Muni's Story," Muni Collection.

55. Brian Aherne, *A Proper Job* (Boston: Houghton Mifflin, 1969), p. 280; Larry Swindell, *Body and Soul: The Story of John Garfield* (New York: Morrow, 1975), p. 142.

56. Lawrence, *Paul Muni*, pp. 242–43; Aherne, *Proper Job*, p. 280; Stine, *Mother Goddam*, p. 116.

and Carlotta; then he shot the Juárez material. Editors never could knit together the two separate pictures. In the editing the royalist half was severely slashed, partially because the movie was too long, but mainly to serve Muni's vanity and to fulfill the rigid contractual control he had over his pictures. Muni felt upstaged by Aherne and Bette Davis. The *New York Times* reported that Muni objected to certain phrases that accorded sympathy to the monarchs and complained that the royal couple was stealing his scenes. Bette Davis summed it up saying, "Muni's seniority proved our downfall," while Aherne claimed that the picture suffered financially because the original title, *The Phantom Crown*, which would have attracted audiences, had been at the last moment changed to *Juárez* to fulfill a clause in Muni's contract, an allegation denied by Muni's biographer. In fact, none of the filmmakers seemed satisfied with the finished project. Even John Garfield, who had fought to become associated with the prestigious film despite being miscast as Díaz, later admitted that his Brooklyn accent hardly enhanced the role.[57]

Following an elaborate publicity campaign, the picture opened with extraordinary fuss and fanfare in April 1939 before a tuxedo-and-tails, special guest audience, including Latin American diplomats, in New York City's Hollywood theater. Rockets' red glare, bombs bursting in air, here was the proof that the flag was still there. Publicity for the movie stressed the contemporary relevance of its theme. Warner Brothers suggested that schools stage debates on the meaning of democracy and oratory contests about the parallels between Louis Napoleon's imperialistic policy in Mexico in 1864 and the predatory politics of the current totalitarian states. The studio urged newspapers to play up the "democracy angle," and the producers proudly called the movie "a contribution to freedom-loving peoples of the world."

The by-invitation-only premiere of *Juárez* was as much a political as a cinematic event. Guests included diplomatic representa-

57. Bette Davis, *The Lonely Life: An Autobiography* (New York: Putnam, 1962), p. 228; Aherne, *Proper Job*, p. 279; Swindell, *John Garfield*, pp. 120, 141; Lawrence, *Paul Muni*, p. 242; *New York Times*, March 12, 1939, sec. 2, p. 5; Jerry Vermilye, *Bette Davis* (New York: Harcourt Brace Jovanovich, 1973), pp. 64–65.

tives from a dozen Latin American countries who arrived in New York City with much fanfare aboard a special train from Washington, D.C. Film notables also attended; this opening was not only a pledge of allegiance to hemispheric unity but a reaffirmation of the wedlock between Hollywood and Washington. Floodlights, champagne—it was an early Fourth of July celebration. Then the inevitable printed reviews began to appear.[58]

It was hard for writers to criticize a picture in which democracy triumphs over dictatorship. In the main they endorsed the call for hemispheric solidarity and supported democracy in its death struggle with fascism. *Newsweek* found the movie "a declaration of faith in the principles of democratic government," and Franz Hollering at *The Nation* urged readers who want "motion pictures which make sense and provide a great experience" to see *Juárez*. *North American Review* praised the new serious trend in filmmaking and proclaimed *Juárez* the best of the lot. The *New York Times* found the movie ideologically faultless, while *Time* generally liked the film, although it mistakenly advised its clientele to pronounce "Juárez" as "Hua-race."[59]

Despite a reluctance to denigrate the movie's *raison d'être*, negative criticism was also strident, although often from partisan quarters. The *New York Times* discovered technical difficulties; the movie simply was not balanced. It broke in two, and while "Juárez is clearly the hero of history, Maximilian is the hero of the picture." *Commonweal*, the Catholic journal, came to the same conclusion and noted further that the picture did not discuss the anticlericalism of Juárez. In a *Commonweal* article that anticipated the release of the picture, Randall Pond sharply criticized the real Juárez, "the so-called democrat," praised Porfirio Díaz, "the admitted dictator," and doubted that the moviemakers would have the courage to tell the truth about the pair. The

58. Swindell, *John Garfield*, p. 143.

59. "The Indian Statesman: Film Life of Juárez a Chapter in the Story of Democracy," *Newsweek*, May 8, 1939, pp. 22–23; Franz Hollering, "Films," *Nation*, May 6, 1939, pp. 539–40; Vance Hall, "Cinema: The Biographical-Historical Trend—Promise of Greater Achievements," *North American Review*, June 1939, p. 379; *New York Times*, April 26, 1939, p. 27; "Juárez," *Time*, May 8, 1939, p. 66.

Communist journal *New Masses* believed that Maximilian "had almost" won the cinematic struggle, while Alan Page, writing for the British cinema publication *Sight and Sound*, thought that the monarch should have emerged victorious. "If he [Maximilian] did have such good ideas, then it was a pity that Juárez should have been so narrow-minded and stupid as to reject his offer of collaboration, since there was every opportunity of establishing a disinterested monarchy such as is enjoyed by this country [England] today." Page evidently had not listened to Juárez's speech, but a colleague at *Sight and Sound*, Herman Weinberg, had. He predicted that the movie might be banned in France, but "Juárez will be a great success in Mexico . . . and that's the most important thing."[60]

A Celluloid "Good Neighbor"

Soon after its gala opening the film was sent on a hemispheric tour as a celluloid ambassador of the Good Neighbor Policy. Mexico's President Cárdenas previewed the film in May and seemed to enjoy it, especially Muni's portrayal of Benito Juárez. Cárdenas made arrangements for the picture's opening in Mexico City's Palace of Fine Arts, the first time that any movie had been so honored. However, presidential endorsement by no means ensured the success of the motion picture in Mexico. A Mexican filmmaker had released a production entitled *Juárez and Maximilian* the previous year, and rumor had it that Warner Brothers had plagiarized from that film. Also, Mexicans disliked "gringos" role playing as their national heroes; they especially had not appreciated the comic antics of Wallace Beery as Pancho Villa in the 1934 picture *Viva Villa!* And the government had heavily censored Sergei Eisenstein's *Thunder over Mexico* because of its failure to capture the feelings and spirit of the Mexican people. Finally, the newspaper *La Prensa*, acting on information provided by friends who had seen *Juárez* in New York City,

60. *New York Times*, April 26, 1939, p. 27; Philip T. Hartung, "Hapsburg in Mexico," *Commonweal*, May 12, 1939, p. 77; Randall Pond, "Juárez and Díaz," *Commonweal*, March 17, 1939, pp. 569–70; *New Masses*, May 11, 1939, p. 28; Alan Page, "Death Always Wins," *Sight and Sound*, Summer 1939, pp. 74–76; Herman G. Weinberg, "Celluloid Trumpet Blasts," *Sight and Sound*, Summer 1939, pp. 58–59.

warned that the movie glorified Maximilian at the expense of Juárez, and that the ending amounted to an outright international effrontery.[61]

Actually, Warner Brothers had considered at least two endings for the picture. In the one selected, Juárez visits the bier of Maximilian and, for dramatic story effect, whispers, "Forgive me," over the body (figure 24). Mexicans thought it scandalous that Juárez in any art form should ask forgiveness from a foreign interloper, and so a good deal of official uneasiness occurred as the film moved toward its conclusion at the Palace of Fine Arts. Then the moment; Muni's lips moved, but he made no sound. The controversial words had been erased from the sound track, and other potentially inflammatory sequences had earlier been removed from the Mexican version of the movie. *Juárez* enjoyed a pleasant opening at the prestigious cultural hall.[62]

Mexico's press, however, was not so generous. Only one newspaper, owned by a prominent labor leader in league with the president, endorsed the picture. *La Prensa* called it "an historical caricature commercially adopted to deceive boobs and persons lacking in genuine affection for Mexico," and in a succession of scathing conclusions noted that the movie "sought to give the impression that the United States felt great love for Mexico sixteen years after it despoiled us of half our territory." Muni's performance reminded them of Frankenstein, and the paper correctly speculated that copies of the film shown in Mexico were not identical to those released in New York.[63]

Ultimas Noticias was scarcely less vituperative. It noted that Warners had tried to sugarcoat the Monroe Doctrine in order to make the "gringo" pill more palatable to Latin Americans, and thought it ludicrous that Juárez carried about Lincoln's picture "like it was his best girl." *Excélsior* found that the personage of Juárez served only as a pretext for the filmmaker to divert the "ideals and doctrines of Yankee absorption" to Europeans, when the real imperialists lay to the north.[64]

61. *New York Times*, July 2, 1939, sec. 9, p. 4; Lawrence, *Paul Muni*, pp. 244–45; SD, 811.4061, Juárez/11.

62. *New York Times*, July 2, 1939, sec. 9, p. 4; Lawrence, *Paul Muni*, pp. 244–45.

63. SD, 811.4061, Juárez/9.

64. SD, 811.4061, Juárez/8, Juárez/10.

Copies of these reviews arrived at the U.S. State Department, which must have wondered about this picture calculated to foment hemispheric unity. Before its release the Latin American desk at the State Department had been bullish on the movie. The Latin Americanists arranged a special showing for ranking members of the department, including Sumner Welles, undersecretary of state, who sent his regrets but wrote Harry Warner that he was pleased by such productions. "I am convinced," he said, "that it contains splendid prospects for the development of a wider appreciation of the historical heritage that is shared jointly by all countries of the New World. Such an appreciation should assist in cementing the very friendly relations which prevail today among those twenty-one republics."[65]

Relations were not nearly as friendly as Sumner Wells supposed, and he probably knew it. Latin American diplomats in Washington, D.C., praised the movie, and their remarks were beamed by shortwave radio to their respective countries. Laurence Duggan, chief of the State Department's Division of American Republics, then decided to use the picture as a test of Latin public opinion toward the United States and hemispheric defense. U.S. embassies and consular stations in Latin America received orders to record audience reaction to the film in their respective districts, and for the next two years the reports filtered in—and many did not augur well for Pan-American cooperation.[66]

Some reports naturally pleased the State Department, especially those from nations with more amicable relations with the United States. Brazil's *Jornal do Brazil* wrote that "the exhibition of *Juárez* in American countries strengthens, through the communion of ideals, the fraternal ties which bind them more and more," while a newspaper in Montevideo, Uruguay, wrote that it could "see the hand of Roosevelt behind the screen, and broad smile of a good neighbor who knows that America does not end

65. Sumner Welles to Harry Warner, May 12, 1939, SD, 811.4061, Juárez/1, Juárez/3, Juárez/3A.

66. Arch Murphy to Ellis O. Briggs, May 6, 1939, SD, 811.4061, Juárez/1, Juárez/5, Juárez/3; Secretary of State of American Diplomatic and Consular Officers in Other American Republics, June 8, 1939, Juárez/6A.

at the Rio Grande and that beyond the Mexican frontier there are millions of men and women devoted to democracy." Students at the University of Chile voted *Juárez* the best film of the year.[67]

But in Veracruz, Mexicans decried Maximilian portrayed as a hero, and Cubans at Cienfuegos saw too much propaganda in the movie. The vice-consul at Santiago de Cuba reported audiences there failed to see any conflict depicted between European imperialism and New World democracy. At Ciudad Trujillo in the Dominican Republic the picture was not well received because it was seen as "out-and-out Yankee propaganda," and because it opposed dictatorship, the form of government with which Dominicans lived. British residents in Panama complained that the film made no distinction between democratic monarchies and totalitarian states. The British minister hoped that Hollywood did not consider all English diplomats as ignorant as the one presented in the movie.[68]

Ecuadorian landowners understandably did not sympathize with an Indian dedicated to land reform who had come to power, and Francophiles in Ecuador thought the debts owed by the Mexicans justified the intervention. Authorities in Lima, Peru, where the government did not permit movies that were either socially significant or unfavorable toward totalitarian powers, banned the film after a ten-week run as a threat to public peace. *Grapes of Wrath* lasted only five days.[69] In sum,

67. U.S. Embassy in Rio de Janeiro to State Department, September 14, 1939, SD, 811.4061, Juárez/37; Dudley G. Dwyre, chargé d'affaires [Montevideo, Uruguay], July 28, 1939, Juárez/24; Claude G. Bowers, ambassador, Santiago, Chile, to secretary of state, December 13, 1939, Juárez/54.

68. William P. Cochran, U.S. consul, Veracruz, Mexico, to secretary of state, March 19, 1940, SD, 811.4061, Juárez/57; American consul in Cienfuegos, Cuba, to State Department, October 24, 1939, Juárez/47; Milton Patterson Thompson, U.S. vice consul in Santiago de Cuba to State Department, February 13, 1940, Juárez/55; Eugene M. Hinkle, interim chargé d'affaires, Ciudad Trujillo, Dominican Republic, to State Department, June 11, 1940, Juárez/65; William Dawson, ambassador, Panama, to State Department, August 19, 1939, Juárez/31; Carlos C. Hall, American consul at Colón, Panama, to secretary of state, August 1, 1939, Juárez/26.

69. Boaz Long, U.S. Legation, Quito, Ecuador, to secretary of state, May 8, 1940, SD, 811.4061, Juárez/63; Mason Turner, consul at Lima, Peru, to State Department, June 18, 1940, Juárez/66.

reports confirmed that Juárez won the cinematic struggle, all right—thanks to the timely intervention of the Monroe Doctrine—but many spectators, yes, diplomats too, even governments sided with the imperialists. It did indeed measure hemispheric opinion. Even when Latins liked the picture, most recognized it as another piece of self-serving propaganda that only underscored the suspicions they already held toward their "good neighbor." So in the end, where *Juárez* may have failed as artistic propaganda, it proved to be a valuable political barometer, and few historical documents better reflect the moral and political dilemma of that anxious period.

A Curtain Call for *Juárez*

Financial and critical returns from the movie disappointed Warner Brothers, but the film had more going against it than its obvious technical and artistic flaws. In 1939 most Americans were either confused by or unconcerned with international events; not many understood the ideological arguments at hand. Even later, more deliberate attempts by the Hollywood-Washington combine to employ movies to arouse a crusade for democracy against totalitarianism left audiences cool. One other crucial factor concerning audience appeal and *Juárez*: a public opinion poll in 1942 showed that Mexicans were the foreign people least appreciated by the American public. Almost sixty percent of the sample questioned found Mexicans "definitely inferior."[70] Under these circumstances, Paul Muni as Juárez the "apelike" Zapotec aborigine could hardly be expected to attract empathy as a heroic defender of democracy. Spectators identified more with the fancy-mannered, more civilized Europeans, Maximilian and Carlotta, despite their political preferences.

Waning profits shelved the picture in the early 1940s, but the movie and its ideological intentions were not forgotten. After World War II, when democracy suffered a new crisis—this time the Russian Stalinists rather than the German and Italian

70. Richard W. Steele, "The Greatest Gangster Movie Ever Filmed: Prelude to War," *Prologue: The Journal of the National Archives*, Winter 1979, pp. 223–24, 227–28, 232–33.

fascists—Warner Brothers re-released the motion picture to do battle against totalitarianism. The fact that former enemies were now not only allies but components of the North Atlantic Treaty Organization Alliance did not deter the studio. Film editors simply removed all former references to the Western European imperialists.[71] They completely eliminated the climactic speech in which Juárez chastises European civilization. No one seemed to miss the crucial sequence except the movie's director, William Dieterle, who noted in 1963 that its absence wrecked the film, because it cut out the justification for the execution of Maximilian. By the time that Dieterle made that observation, *Juárez* had for some time been taken from general circulation. The director, however, suggested another re-release. He thought the picture especially timely for the 1960s when guerrillas in Vietnam were putting up such heroic resistance against another great, imperialistic army.[72] Studio records reveal no response to that recommendation.

My sincere gratitude goes to my colleagues Rosalie Schwartz, a Latin Americanist and film specialist, and Richard T. Ruetten and Richard W. Steele, specialists in contemporary United States history, for their careful reading of this essay and their recommendations, which greatly improved it. I also wish to dedicate my part of this book to my buddy, Glenn Louis Syktich.

71. "Revisions of Reels 6 and 7," June 1, 1952, Production Materials Number 59, *Juárez*, Warner Brothers Studios.

72. Tom Flinn, "William Dieterle: The Plutarch of Hollywood," *Velvet Light Trap*, Fall 1975, p. 28.

1. *Claude Rains, as the haughty imperialist Louis Napoleon, evaluates democracy: "The rule of the cattle by the cattle for the cattle."*

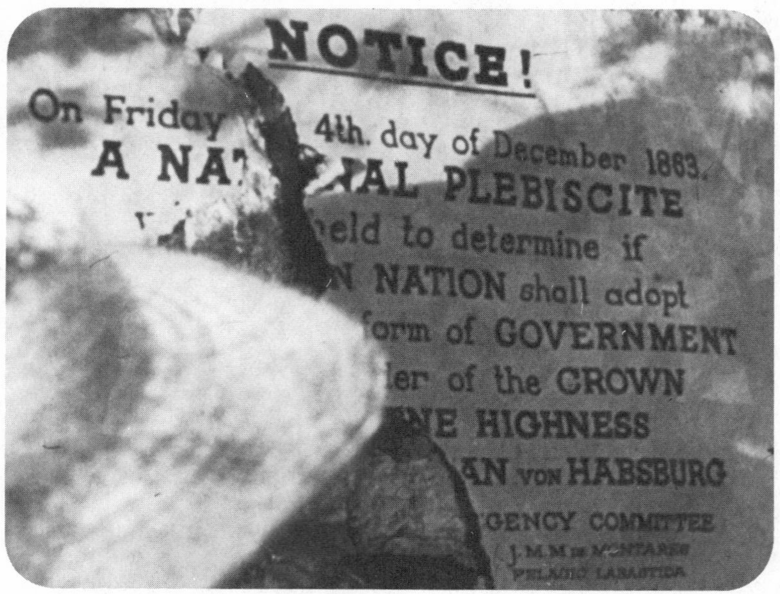

2. *Director William Dieterle, a believer in omens, photographed this brief scene separately so that filming would begin on a date with favorable celestial signs.*

3. *Although the historical connection never existed, the filmmakers visually tied Juárez to Lincoln with correspondence and backdrops.*

4. *The patriotic followers of Juárez, bathed in heroic lighting, pose as if chipped from Mount Rushmore.*

5. *Screenwriter Aeneas MacKenzie saw Juárez as an "apelike aborigine," a Pithecanthropus—an emergence of mentality from matter.*

6. *The glamorous arrival of Carlotta and Maximilian to Mexico established sympathy for the tragic couple, despite their ideological aversion to democracy.*

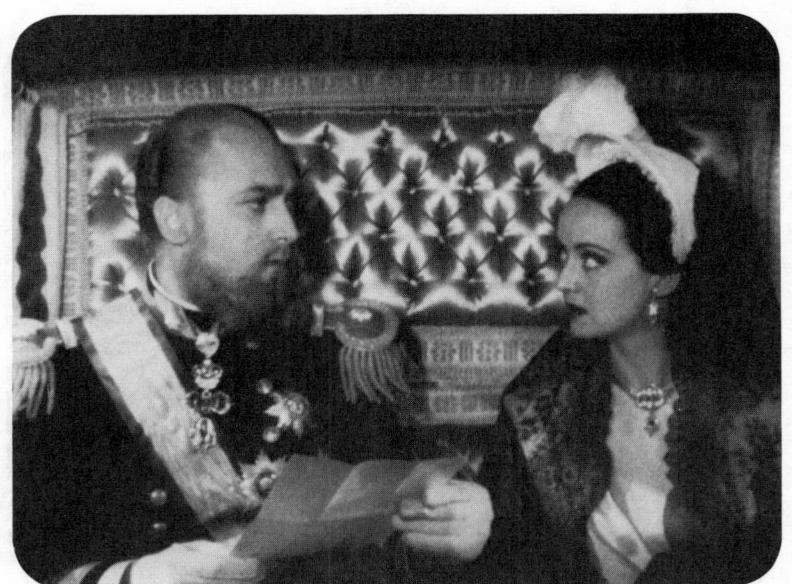

7. *A letter from Juárez warns the handsome and sensitive royal couple that they are the dupes of power-hungry European dictators.*

8. *Flat lighting accentuates the benign, even fragile, qualities of Maximilian, an amateur artist as well as a benevolent monarch.*

9. *Juárez, harassed by French troops, cannot leave Lincoln behind (note the spotlight on the portrait).*

10. *Pepe, in style and manner, becomes cinema's stereotypic Mexican in explaining guerrilla warfare to Juárez.*

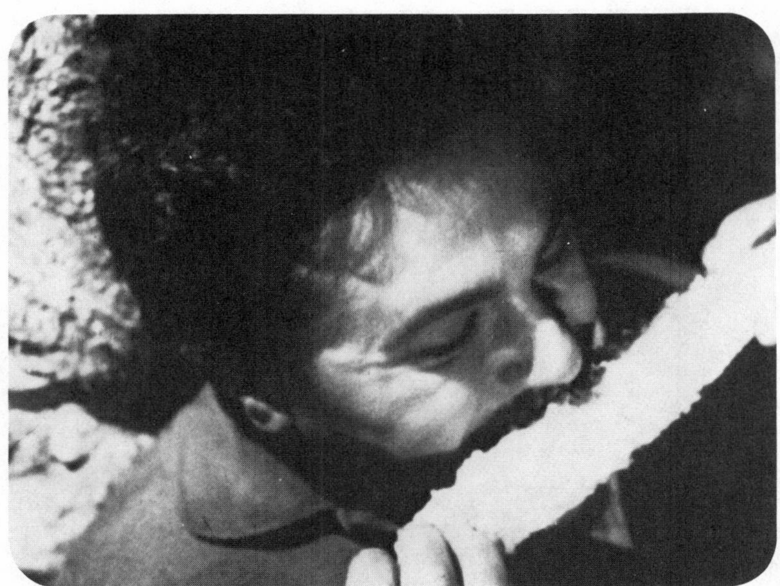

11. *Dieterle insisted upon authenticity in details, if not in history. Here John Garfield eats genuine Mexican corn, purchased at excessive cost for the film.*

12. *A heavenly, childish innocence is imputed to Bette Davis and Brian Aherne by lighting typical of the period.*

13. *Juárez teaches Porfirio Díaz the difference between democracy and monarchy as Lincoln looks on.*

14. *Imagery enlisted God on the side of the republicans (the Western Hemisphere) in their struggle against totalitarians.*

15. *Goya's famous* Dos de Mayo *was visually borrowed to substantiate the classical martyrdom of freedom lovers in their battle against interventionists.*

16. *The faces of Mexico—the endless patience, determination, and agony of the oppressed everywhere—gave the picture an eternal touch.*

17. *The U.S. ambassador warns Louis (here posing for a portraitist) that the Monroe Doctrine is about to knock him from his high horse.*

18. *Carlotta departs to demand European assistance. Her clothing has turned to gray, signifying her failing political fortunes and mental decline.*

19. *Juárez, man of the people, although hardly dressed as a campesino, arrives in top hat and with briefcase to challenge a political adversary.*

20. *Bette Davis's famous angry stare is turned upon Louis Napoleon, who has abandoned his Mexican adventure.*

21. *Muni ponders Maximilian's fate as Lincoln provides inspiration and guidance.*

22. *While seeking to discredit his politics, the filmmakers persistently portrayed Maximilian in sympathetic images, here listening to a Mexican love song.*

23. *Carlotta, now dressed in black to signify her total political defeat and mental collapse, longs for Maximilian in a series of romantic images.*

24. *Muni at the bier of Maximilian murmurs, "Forgive me," but not in the version released in Mexico, where audiences protested that their revered president would never ask forgiveness of an interloper.*

Juárez

Screenplay

by

JOHN HUSTON

AENEAS MacKENZIE

and

WOLFGANG REINHARDT

Characters in the Action which occurs between July 1863 and June 1867

Imperialists

Napoleon III	Emperor of France
Eugenie	His wife; empress of France
Duc de Morny	Illegitimate brother and adviser of Napoleon III
Drouyn de Lhuys	Minister of state to Napoleon III
Marshal Randon	Minister of war to Napoleon III
Achille Fould	Minister of finance to Napoleon III
Maximilian von Hapsburg	Archduke of Austria, later emperor of Mexico
Carlotta	His wife
Countess Kollonitz	Lady-in-waiting to Carlotta
José María Manuel de Montares (composite or fictional character)	Leader of the reactionary party in Mexico
Dr. Samuel Basch	Physician-in-ordinary to Maximilian
Achille Bazaine	Maréchal of France, commander of the French armies in Mexico
Major Dupont (composite or fictional character)	Maréchal's political officer, a general staff type, wearing pince-nez
Velazquez de León	A reactionary minister in Maximilian's council

Mariano Salas	Member of the Mexican Regency Committee
Pelagio Labastida	Archbishop of Mexico
Colonel Miguel López	Maximilian's Mexican aide-de-camp
Prince Salm-Salm	Maximilian's European aide-de-camp
Tomás Mejía	Maximilian's Indian general
Miguel Miramón	Maximilian's Mexican general
Agustín de Iturbide	Adopted child of Maximilian and Carlotta
Senator Harris, Hartman, Roberts	Three Americans
A painter	At the court of Napoleon III

Juaristas

Benito Juárez	Constitutional president of Mexico
Porfirio Díaz	General in the army of the republic
Alejandro Rodriguez Uradi (composite or fictional character)	Vice-president of the republic
Mariano Escobedo	Republican general
Riva Palacio	Republican general
Regules	Republican general
Carbajal	Republican general
Corona	Republican general
Rivera	Republican general
Lerdo de Tejada	Secretary of state to Juárez

Diplomats

Baron von Magnus	Prussian ambassador to Mexico
Sir Peter Campbell-Scarlett	British ambassador to Mexico
John Bigelow	U.S. ambassador to France
Prince Richard Metternich	Austrian ambassador to France

French soldiers, Mexican soldiers, peons, priest, various palace officials and servants

Juárez

NOTE: The following "Napoleon scene" will be preceded by a prologue establishing and showing in several alternating "tableaux" the contrasting careers of Juárez and Maximilian from their birth to manhood.

There will be no dialogue spoken by the characters shown in these "silent" scenes, but a narrator's voice will explain them.

The Napoleon scene is, therefore, the first scene of the picture in which the actors actually talk, and consequently through its development our main protagonists are brought into story contact.[1]

1–11. LONG SHOT A RUGGED MEXICAN LANDSCAPE

Against a dramatic background of mountains and clouds we see a Zapotec[2] Indian village nestled in the shadows of the valley. A narrator's voice comes over the scene:

NARRATOR'S VOICE:

Mexico—vast, silent, ominous— In the church of the Indian village of Ixtlán,[3] in the early part of the nineteenth century—

DISSOLVE TO:

12. MED. SHOT EXT. THE CHURCH

It is a dilapidated adobe structure surmounted by a crude cross. Its solitary bell peals as the narrator's voice continues:

NARRATOR'S VOICE:

—a boy child of a Zapotec Indian father and mother is being baptized.

DISSOLVE TO:

13. INT. THE CHURCH MED. SHOT AT ALTAR

Under the flickering light of the altar candles a Mexican priest is baptizing an Indian baby. Its parents and grandparents watch silently as the priest bathes the tiny head of the boy with holy water, puts a little salt on his lips, and finally anoints him with oil. The narrator's voice comes in with:

NARRATOR'S VOICE:

In the register of the parochial church of Saint Thomas of Ixtlán a name is written—

DISSOLVE TO:

14. INSERT REGISTER OF BIRTHS

In the middle of the page, above which is written the text of the notice of baptism, a pen in the hand of the priest writes as the voice of the narrator reads.

VOICE OF NARRATOR:

—Benito Juárez, son of Marcelino Juárez and Brigida García. (As the camera irises down to the name of Benito Juárez the narrator's voice continues.) In another country—in another church—another boy child is being baptized.

DISSOLVE TO:

15. INT. SAINT STEPHEN'S CATHEDRAL IN VIENNA

MED. SHOT THE HIGH ALTAR

In contrast to the primitive simplicity of the little Mexican church we see the Gothic splendor of Saint Stephen's.[4] An archbishop in full robes performs the baptismal ceremony. The parents and grandparents, splendid in court dress, watch proudly. At a respectful distance are gathered the aristocracy of Austria. The camera moves to a

16. CLOSER SHOT AT ALTAR

The archbishop sprinkles the head of the blond, blue-eyed baby[5] with holy water, then puts the salt on its lips. As he starts to anoint the baby the voice of the narrator comes in with:

VOICE OF NARRATOR:

In the register of Saint Stephen's Cathedral in Vienna a name is also written—

DISSOLVE TO:

17. INSERT REGISTER

Under the text of the baptism the pen in the hand of the archbishop writes as the voice of the narrator reads:

VOICE OF NARRATOR:

—Ferdinand Maximilian Joseph, archduke of Austria, son of Sophia and Karl Joseph. (As the camera irises down on the name of Maximilian the narrator continues.) In the shadows of the towering Sierra Madres the little Indian baby grew up to be a sturdy stripling of a lad.

DISSOLVE TO:

18. MED. SHOT EXT. A SUN-DRENCHED FIELD

A flock of sheep graze idly. In the shadow of a tree a barefooted Indian boy of twelve is stretched on his stomach, his head in his hands, painfully deciphering the words of a book. Over scene, from a distance, come the happy notes of a shepherd's pipe.

NARRATOR'S VOICE (continuing):

Unlike the other shepherd boys little Benito was not content to whittle himself a reed flute to while away the time. He wanted to learn—learn the strange Spanish tongue he heard spoken in the nearby towns . . . no small task, for there were neither books nor teachers in the village of San Pablo Guelatao . . . But in Vienna—in the Palace of Schönbrunn—[6]

DISSOLVE TO:

19. MED. CLOSE SHOT INT. AN ORNATE STUDY IN THE SCHÖNBRUNN PALACE

Its walls are lined with books. Three or four tutors are in attendance on the boy Maximilian, patiently instructing him in the intricacies of some court ceremony. As we come into the scene the narrator's voice continues:

NARRATOR'S VOICE:

—there are many books and many teachers for the young Archduke Maximilian von Hapsburg. Because he was a Hapsburg he had to learn early the prerogatives of a sovereign—the elaborate ceremonials of monarchy—its intricate precedents and procedures—for someday Maximilian might have to rule Austria. For his years of dutiful application and zeal Maximilian was rewarded. Upon him was conferred the Order of the Knight of the Golden Fleece—[7]

DISSOLVE TO:

20. INT. THRONE ROOM IN THE SCHÖNBRUNN PALACE

MED. SHOT DAIS

We see the ceremony of conferring the Order of the Golden Fleece (MacKenzie will furnish detail) on Maximilian, now a full-grown young man. (See picture in Harding, p. 14.)[8] The narrator's voice continues.

NARRATOR'S VOICE:

—the patent of the highest nobility—the hallmark of a king—a title that was inalienably his by right of birth. For his years of undaunted persistence and implacable will—Benito Juárez was also rewarded. Upon him was conferred—

DISSOLVE TO:

21. MED. SHOT INT. A LECTURE HALL IN THE INSTITUTE OF ARTS AND SCIENCES AT OAXACA[9]

In contrast to the ornate throne room, the hall is bare and severe in its furnishings. It is crowded with students and their relatives. On the platform is gathered the faculty of the institute, robed in academic caps and gowns. The president is in the speaker's rostrum. Juárez, a full-grown young man, stands before him in a simple bachelor's gown. The president hands Juárez his diploma and then shakes hands with him. As we come into the scene the narrator's voice continues with:

NARRATOR'S VOICE:

—the degree of bachelor of law. But the times were not propitious for a lawyer—even a brilliant lawyer . . . Mexico was in turmoil . . .

The camera moves to a:

22. CLOSE SHOT THE FLAG OF THE REPUBLIC OF MEXICO hanging on the wall behind the platform.

NARRATOR'S VOICE (continuing):

There had been fifty-two revolutions in the forty years that Mexico had been a republic. Revolution and counterrevolution followed with sickening regularity.[10] The patriots of Mexico were appalled. A small group gathered in a meeting . . .

DISSOLVE TO:

23. MED. CLOSE SHOT INT. A ROOM NIGHT
lighted by a single oil lamp on a table. Grouped around it are a number of men, their faces tense and grim as they sit in silence.

NARRATOR'S VOICE (continuing):

Something must be done—and done immediately! A man is needed—a man to lead Mexico out of chaos! (One of the group, an old man, rises slowly. All eyes go to him. He addresses the group. The voice of the narrator is synchronized so that he speaks the words of the old man.) I will show you that man . . .

The old man takes the lamp from the table and crosses with it to the far corner of the room, the camera moving with him. As he stops the light of the lamp reveals a face, impassive as stone. It is the face of Benito Juárez, now a man of thirty-five ([Paul] Muni). The camera moves up to a

24. CLOSE SHOT JUÁREZ
The voice of the narrator continues over scene:

VOICE OF NARRATOR:

In 1857 Benito Juárez became president of the Republic of Mexico. He faced an almost superhuman task. The country was devastated . . .[11]

DISSOLVE TO:

25. EXT. A FIELD
neglected and choked with weeds. Here and there a withered cornstalk waves in the breeze. In the background the blackened ruins of a burned-out farmhouse.

VOICE OF NARRATOR (continuing):

The mass of its people starved and hopeless . . .

DISSOLVE TO:

26. SEVERAL CLOSE SHOTS OF PEONS
their faces gaunt as they sit with their women and children, staring in the stupor of their hunger.

VOICE OF NARRATOR (continuing):

Mexico was bankrupt—not only morally but financially. Her debts to foreign nations had been piled to fantastic heights. The situation was desperate. It called for bold measures. Juárez signed a decree—

DISSOLVE TO:

27. INT. OFFICE OF THE PRESIDENT IN THE NATIONAL PALACE
We see Juárez at his desk, signing a paper as the voice of the narrator continues:

VOICE OF NARRATOR:

—declaring a moratorium on foreign debts. England and Spain agreed to wait. Only France objected. Her emperor, Napoleon the Third, used this as a pretext to further his imperial ambitions.[12] In 1863 his troops invaded Mexico.

DISSOLVE TO:

28. EXT. A COUNTRY ROAD

With drums rolling, French columns are moving forward, complete with artillery and supply trains.

The voice of the narrator continues:

VOICE OF NARRATOR:

Even while preparing to meet force with force, Juárez pushed his plans for the rehabilitation of Mexico. He struck at the root of her major evil—the concentration of her lands in the hands of a small but powerful group of landowners. A law was passed enabling Juárez to distribute these lands among the peons . . .

DISSOLVE TO:

29. AN OPEN FIELD

A long line of peons stretches up to a rough, wooden table set up in the field. Juárez and a corps of assistants are busy at the table signing and sealing the deeds which Juárez gives to each peon as he steps to the table before him.[13]

VOICE OF NARRATOR (continuing):

The landowners watched, sullen and resentful . . . (The camera moves to a group of landowners gathered around the shiny black carriage of Montares.) For the moment they were powerless . . . But there must be some way of stopping the hateful Indian and his dangerous laws. There must be someone who would join hands with them to destroy Benito Juárez . . . There was—Louis Napoleon—emperor of France.

DISSOLVE TO:

29A. CLOSE SHOT THE SIGNET OF THE HOUSE OF BONAPARTE THE LETTER N

surrounded by an imperial crown. The camera moves back to:

30. MED. SHOT INT. COUNCIL CHAMBER IN THE TUILERIES with Napoleon and Eugenie at the head of a large table, flanked by the ministers de Morny, Randon, de Lhuys, Fould, and others. The emperor is addressing a tall, swarthy gentleman of Latin appearance.

NAPOLEON:

Señor Montares, it is absurd to consider the restoration of lands in Mexico—even in occupied territory—before the entire country has been subdued . . . You and your fellow members of the Mexican Conservative Party must have patience . . . as we ourselves must have patience . . . until Maréchal Bazaine has put an end to republican resistance.[14]

He turns as the secretary comes up to him with the dispatch in his hand.

SECRETARY:

A most urgent dispatch from the ambassador in Washington, Your Imperial Majesty.

Napoleon opens the communication and commences to read. At a startled oath, "Sapristi,"[15] Eugenie looks over his shoulder to inspect the text for her own information.

CUT TO:

31. INSERT DISPATCH
It reads:

French Embassy
Washington, D.C.
July 4th, 1863

To H.I.M. the emperor Napoleon III
Paris
The Confederate Army of General Lee was decisively beaten at Gettysburg on July the third and is now in full retreat.

It is the unanimous opinion of military experts here that this defeat terminates all prospects of final victory for the southern states.

Full details of the situation will follow by the next packet.

A. Mercier
Ambassador

CUT TO:

32. MED. CLOSE SHOT NAPOLEON, EUGENIE, AND NEARBY MINISTERS

EUGENIE:

What does this mean to us, Louis?

NAPOLEON (sarcastically):

What does it mean? The American Civil War may end at any moment, and the North is going to win! What do you think it means? (Tossing the dispatch to Maréchal Randon.)

EUGENIE:

But we—

NAPOLEON:

We undertook the conquest of Mexico on the theory that the South would be victorious and that a divided America would be unable to enforce the Monroe Doctrine. (There is shocked silence among the ministers as Napoleon rises and begins to pace the room like an angry lion. He stops before the minister of war, who is sitting numbed with the dispatch in his hand.) You are responsible for this, Randon . . . You convinced us that the South was certain to triumph!

RANDON:

This Battle of Gettysburg is incomprehensible . . .

NAPOLEON:

It is your business as minister of war to know which

side will win a battle *before* it is fought. (He resumes his march across the floor of the chamber.) The Second Empire is finished . . . doomed . . . destroyed . . . because I listened to fools. (He looks at the various ministers insultingly.) Fools! Fools!

RANDON:

I admit my mistake, Your Majesty.

NAPOLEON:

Mistake! "Mistake" you call it! I cannot afford the luxury of such things as mistakes . . . Mistakes are for constitutional monarchs, presidents, and such like . . . not for a supreme autocrat! (At the end of his beat before the table, he reverses his steps regularly, in the same furious stride.) Millions have been poured into the Mexican conquest . . . millions for men and more men—ships—munitions. I could have conquered half of Europe at less cost. (He stops, whirls on his heel to face them, and grinds out the coal of his cigarette on the polished table. Continuing, to de Morny.) You and your banker friends got me into this mess . . .

DE MORNY:

Your Majesty is unfair . . . The collection of Mexico's debt was of secondary importance . . . Your Majesty intervened in Mexico to block the spread of American democracy.

NAPOLEON:

Democracy! The rule of the cattle by the cattle for the cattle . . . Abraham Lincoln—bah! Parliaments and plebiscites and proletarians— A mob intoxicated with ideas of equality—cattle! (He almost foams at the mouth.) Well, am I to be destroyed by such filth . . . Am I? (He looks from one minister to another, each of whom evades his glare and turns questioning eyes on the remaining members of the council, with no results.) Well, what do you advise now: Shall we evacuate Mexico . . . permit the humiliation of French imperialism by Benito Juárez—an Indian bandit! . . . and be engulfed by a revolution here at home? Or shall we wait for the Yankees to destroy us on the Rio Grande?

DE MORNY:
If we evacuate Mexico now, we are certain to have trouble here at home. As I see it, there is everything to lose by an immediate withdrawal.

NAPOLEON (raging):
No doubt that is the way you *do* see it, de Morny. (He glares around the council for an answer, with no results.)

EUGENIE:
Calm yourself, Louis. We have no great problem in this affair.

NAPOLEON (about to proceed with his bellowings, but checking himself and looking at the empress as do all the others):
Does Madame imply that she sees a solution?

EUGENIE:
Take a lesson from your uncle, Louis. How did the first Napoleon hold Holland? By giving Holland a monarch! How did he hold Sweden? By giving Sweden a monarch. Why shouldn't you hold Mexico in the same way . . . by giving Mexico a monarch of its own.[16]

NAPOLEON (stopping suddenly in his tracks):
But the Monroe Doctrine—

EUGENIE (interrupting):
The Monroe Doctrine applies only to the taking of American territory by European powers, not to the internal affairs of American nations. Consequently the United States would have no legal grounds for

complaint were Mexico to have an emperor—who happened to favor French interests.[17]

There is a moment or two of complete silence in which the men look from one to the other. Napoleon then turns his eye from the empress to de Morny, who nods in final assurance.

DE MORNY:

Someone who would agree to reimburse us for the cost of occupation and guarantee the payment of our Mexican loans.[18]

FOULD:

To say nothing of making substantial commercial concessions. In short, messieurs, someone who would provide us with the profit of a colony and relieve us of its responsibilities.

EUGENIE:

Of course, the request for a sovereign must come from the Mexican nation itself.

DE MORNY (to Montares):

No doubt the gentlemen of the Mexican Conservative Party whom Señor Montares represents will be overjoyed at the prospect of a monarch.

MONTARES (grimly):

A monarch who would return to us the lands which were seized by Benito Juárez.

NAPOLEON (chewing the tube of his cigarette):

Hmm . . . (He now walks very slowly up and down the length of the table, then stops, looks at Eugenie, and smiles. The ministers sigh in unanimous relief as they watch him commence to assume the role of a polished and ingratiating Frenchman.) Excellent, my dear, excellent! (To the council.) Messieurs, since the idea originated with Madame l'Impératrice, it shall be her privilege to nominate the future emperor of Mexico!

There is a chorus of approval and bows from the ministers in the direction of Eugenie.

EUGENIE (with all the gusto of a barmaid's daughter for the situation):

Then let us see . . . (Tapping her fan stick against her lips.) There's Prince Albrecht of Anhalt-Zerbst —but he's a Protestant, of course, and won't do . . . The Margrave Carl of Lippe-Detmold—too old . . . The Duke of Modena—too fat . . .[19]

DE MORNY:

And all of them obvious puppets, madame.

EUGENIE (after further thought; to Napoleon):

Louis, we need a prince of great name . . . a name so great that its bearer will be recognized automatically by the powers of Europe . . . The name of an ancient, ruling house.

DISSOLVE TO:

33. INSERT

The complete heraldic achievement of the House of Hapsburg-Lorraine, with its supporters, mantling, and crests.

DISSOLVE TO:

34. THE TERRACE OF THE MARBLE PALACE OF MIRAMAR

near Trieste.[20] It stands on a low point of the coast, seagirt by the waters of the Adriatic on three sides, in a setting of idyllic beauty.

Maximilian von Hapsburg is at an easel, engaged in an attempt to capture the seascape on canvas. The results are rather unfortunate. Weary at last, he lowers his brush and stands gazing aimlessly out over the waters until he hears the step of his young wife, the lovely archduchess Carlotta, then he resumes his work immediately. Carlotta comes to his side, looks first at the canvas, then out to sea.

CARLOTTA (pointing):
See that dark cloud gathering beyond the promontory . . .

MAXIMILIAN:
We must be going to have a thundershower.

CARLOTTA:
Max'l, why do storms always come out of the west?

MAXIMILIAN:
The Gulf Stream is the reason, I believe. It brings warm waters from the Gulf of Mexico to our Atlantic coasts, where they vaporize and form clouds which are blown in by the west winds.[21] (He applies another color to the canvas and stands back to see the effect. It doesn't please him.) If only I could paint what I see. I mix a color— (he demonstrates) it seems to be all right on the palette, but on canvas, next to another color, it isn't right at all . . . no, not at all.

CARLOTTA:
I think you paint exceedingly well, Max'l, considering the fact that you've never had any lessons.

MAXIMILIAN (smiling):
My painting is abominable. But I don't really care. I paint because it teaches one to look closer into nature and see more of its beauties.

CARLOTTA:
You have a talent for discerning beauty where no one else would think of looking.

MAXIMILIAN (tenderly):
Such pleasures are the result of contentment—the tranquility and peace of mind which came to me with you, Liebchen . . . (Kisses her.) How fortunate we are in being here together at Miramar, away from the formalities and regimentations of a court.

CARLOTTA:

Max'l—honestly! Do you never miss the excitement of being in the center of things? Of taking your part in affairs of state again? Do you never feel the necessity for achievement?

MAXIMILIAN:

Was appearing at state functions beside my brother, Franz Josef—or rather, one step to the left and two steps behind him—an achievement? Was dressing in my grand admiral's uniform and reviewing the fleet an achievement? I believe in our lives here with all my heart. I am proud of causing the *hibiscus syriacus*[22] to bloom this far north. That, madame, is an achievement which counts. (He sits down and resumes his painting determinedly while Carlotta stands looking at him in some silent speculation. Suddenly he lays aside his brushes.) It must be time for the post, Carla.

CARLOTTA:

Yes, Max'l, I put it on the table.

She takes his arm and they stroll around a corner of the palace toward a wicker table laid with a silver tea and coffee service.

CARLOTTA (looking up from a letter, headed Royal Palace, Brussels):

Henriette and Leopold are in London . . .[23] (Bubbling with laughter.) Imagine, Max'l, Victoria has Cousin Albert in Scotch kilts . . . ! And he's afraid to sit down in them. (Maximilian smiles in answer and turns back to his own reading.) Henriette and Leopold send you their love.

MAXIMILIAN (referring to the letter in his own hand):

And my mother inquires after your health.

35. INSERT THE LETTER

from the Hofburg Palace,[24] which Maximilian is holding. It reads:

> How is dear Charlotte? Is she in good health? We are hoping to hear after three years of disappointment that you are now looking forward to the arrival of an heir.

CUT TO:

36. BACK TO SCENE

CARLOTTA:

What else does your mother say, Max'l?

MAXIMILIAN:

Oh, nothing.

He puts the letter aside, picks up a newspaper, unwraps it, and begins to read. Suddenly he scowls. Carlotta, happening to glance up, is surprised at his expression.

CARLOTTA:

What is it, Max'l?

MAXIMILIAN:

The Czech delegates walked out of the Imperial Assembly in protest. Franz Josef is going to take repressive measures . . .[25] (Throwing the paper to the floor.) Will he never learn that loyalty is not to be enforced? (Rising and walking a few steps.) My brother is a fool . . . ! His absolutism is medieval . . . An alien race can be won only by benevolence.

CARLOTTA:

What a pity, Max'l, that you are not in your brother's place . . . *You* would be the enlightened ruler of the future. Oh, it is a shame that your great gifts should be denied to a world that has such need of them.

MAXIMILIAN:

Sometimes I wonder if Europe's ailments are not far

graver than anyone imagines. Can the hates and prejudices of this ancient civilization ever be reconciled? Or must all its traditions be uprooted . . . ? Must it die to be reborn?[26] (Smiling at her in a sudden change of mood.) Meantime, however, we have our *hibiscus syriacus* . . . (Seeing Carlotta's lady-in-waiting enter scene.) Yes, Countess?

COUNTESS KOLLONITZ:
A relative whom I have not seen for several years has just arrived in Trieste, Your Serene Highness, and I wondered if you could find it possible to afford him the distinction of being presented.

MAXIMILIAN:
Indeed, Countess. You must bring him to dinner with us tonight. (To Carlotta.) We are dining *en famille* this evening, are we not?

CARLOTTA:
Yes, Max'l, quite informally—with Dr. Basch.

MAXIMILIAN:
Excellent! Then we shall look forward to seeing you both. What is the gentleman's name?

KOLLONITZ:
Señor José María Manuel de Montares.

MAXIMILIAN:
A Spaniard, Countess?

KOLLONITZ:
No, Serene Highness—a Mexican.

As Carlotta looks up to the sky and stretches her hand out to feel the first drop of rain

DISSOLVE TO:

37. THE DINING ROOM AT MIRAMAR MAXIMILIAN, CARLOTTA, KOLLONITZ, BASCH, AND MONTARES at a perfectly appointed table, during a game course.

Liveried servants move silently in the background. The sound of rain beating against the windows can be heard.

MAXIMILIAN:

You must try our fifty-two Metternich, Señor Montares. It's an excellent year . . . (After the butler has filled Montares's glass.) What are your wines in Mexico?

MONTARES:

Most of our plants have been imported from Europe, Serene Highness.

MAXIMILIAN:

And may I ask how they prosper in the tropical soil?

MONTARES:

They produce exceedingly well, but the character of the wine undergoes a change, becoming heavier and stronger . . . I can tell you a curious fact. Your Highness of course knows how a wine in the bottle is affected by the change of seasons, becoming cloudy and disturbed at certain periods of the year. Well, in Mexico, the wines produced from imported plants do not respond to our seasons but to the seasons of the lands from which they came.

CARLOTTA:

Extraordinary!

MAXIMILIAN (in pleased challenge to the physician):

And how does a scientist like Dr. Basch explain that phenomenon?

DR. BASCH:

Wine, Your Highness, is a living thing. It is because it responds to the seasons that it grows old in a bottle.

MAXIMILIAN:

But why doesn't it respond to the seasons of Mexico rather than to the seasons of lands thousands of miles distant?

DR. BASCH:

Because no matter how far the plants are carried, something of France or Germany or Spain—their sun, their soil, their seasons—will remain in the vine and wine from the vine forever.[27]

MAXIMILIAN (raising his glass):

Your good health, señor. (Maximilian drinks.)

Montares raises his glass, holds it to the light, turns it around, inhales the bouquet, and tastes the wine in all the ritual of a connoisseur.

MONTARES:

Superb, Your Serene Highness.

CARLOTTA:

Señor Montares, is it true that Mexico has had some fifty revolutions since she proclaimed her independence?

MONTARES (grimly):

Fifty-two revolutions in forty years . . . Your Highness, Mexico is a very rich country: gold, silver, copper, and this new petroleum oil abound; tobacco, cocoa, and spices; amber and coral and pearls . . .[28] (He sighs.) And her wealth has made Mexico prey of unprincipled men . . . adventurers, serving their passion for money and power.

MAXIMILIAN:

And how do they find their followings, these adventurers?

MONTARES:

In the case of Benito Juárez, for example, by intoxicating the ignorant peon class with lies and promises.

MAXIMILIAN:

What do these lies and promises consist of?

MONTARES:

Juárez is a power-mad demagogue— His is the gospel of destruction . . . He attacks civilization . . . all authority! I myself am among his victims . . . All my estates he seized—the lands that my family owned for generations.

KOLLONITZ:

How awful!

MAXIMILIAN:

The failure of Mexico, of course, lies in the attempt to govern herself by the democratic principle—which is the last refinement of a social concept—far, far beyond the capacity of any people today. And for a young nation like Mexico . . . (He gestures its futility.)

MONTARES:

In my own opinion, the sole hope for Mexico is that some European prince of great name will consent to rule over the nation as an emperor. (Carlotta looks up at him quickly.)

CARLOTTA:

Is there a tendency in that direction among the people?

MONTARES:

A pronounced tendency, Your Serene Highness—even on the part of the liberal element.

Carlotta and Basch exchange glances.

CARLOTTA:

Did you have any audiences with the emperor Napoleon while you were in Paris?

MONTARES:

Yes, Your Serene Highness. As a member of the Mexican Regency Committee we had numerous conferences.

CARLOTTA:

And is he, too, in favor of establishing a monarchy?

MONTARES:

Completely, Your Highness, provided a suitable candidate can be found: Someone who can become a symbol to the Mexican people . . . combining great talent with a great name . . . (After a pause; to Maximilian in the most graceful tones.) Why should Your Serene Highness not interest himself on behalf of my fatherland? May I remind Your Serene Highness that Hernando Cortés came to Mexico in the name of your illustrious ancestor, Charles the Fifth.

CARLOTTA:

Señor Montares, am I mistaken in the impression that you are here to afford us something more than your entertaining and instructive company?

MONTARES (after a pronounced pause):

Your Serene Highness is quite correct. (Turning toward Maximilian.) I am here on behalf of my country and the emperor Napoleon the Third, to ascertain informally if the archduke Ferdinand Maximilian von Hapsburg will consider an offer of the Mexican crown to himself and the heirs of his body.

38. CLOSE-UP CARLOTTA

as she blazes with contained emotions, looking at no one but seeing far beyond the walls of Miramar. Then her head turns quickly in the direction of Maximilian, and her eyes fix on him.

39. GROUP SHOT MAXIMILIAN, CARLOTTA, MONTARES

MAXIMILIAN (his expression profoundly serious; after a period of thought):

Before taking so grave a matter into consideration, I

should have to acquaint myself with all the circumstances surrounding the offer. There would have to be a plebiscite, of course, to determine the free will of the Mexican people.

DISSOLVE TO:

40. INSERT A PRINTED NOTICE IN SPANISH
nailed to a door. Translated by transposition, it reads:

NOTICE

On Friday, the fourth day of December, 1863, a NATIONAL PLEBISCITE will be held to determine if the MEXICAN NATION shall adopt a MONARCHIAL FORM OF GOVERNMENT and make tender of the CROWN to His Serene Highness THE ARCHDUKE MAXIMILIAN VON HAPSBURG.

By order of
THE REGENCY COMMITTEE[29]
José María Manuel de Montares
Monsignor Pelagio Labastida
Mariano Salas

DISSOLVE TO:

41. DOOR OF AN ADOBE HOVEL
at which a French corporal and private are knocking. As it opens pan with them to the interior where a peon and an old woman are seated on petates eating a meager meal of tortillas.

CORPORAL:
What is your name?

PEON:
I am Angel Almengo.

The private writes it on a sheet of paper tacked to a board, which he hands to the peon.

CORPORAL:
Make your mark . . . (pointing) here! (The peon

marks and returns the board to the private.) What is your father's name?

PEON:

Doreato Almengo.

The private writes and hands back the board again.

CORPORAL:

Mark here!

PEON:

But my father is dead, señor.

CORPORAL:

Mark here!

As the peon does

DISSOLVE TO:

42. AN ASSEMBLY OF PEONS AND POORER-CLASS TOWNSFOLK listening to a speaker who is standing on a bench in a public plaza.

SPEAKER:

You are being tricked, compañeros . . . Do not write your names or make your marks . . . The paper says we want an emperor to come from Europe and rule over us . . . We do not want an emperor. We have a president, Benito Juárez, who helped us poor peons to get lands to farm . . . If an emperor comes, he will take them away. Then we shall starve and be slaves again . . .

A clatter of hoofs begins to sound over the scene. The listeners turn, break, and run in all directions as soldiers ride over them and close in on the speaker.

DISSOLVE TO:

43. CONTINUATION OF SCENE 42
This scene has already been shot. The speaker has said that he will not sign the plebiscite; he has run out of the shot and up the stairway; he has yelled, "Viva

Juárez—Viva la República!" The French soldier has lifted his revolver, and the peon, mortally wounded, has fallen dead over the railing of the balcony.

DISSOLVE TO:

44. EXT. PLAZA DARKENED CITY OF SALTILLO NIGHT

Truck shot past shadowy sentries before the single lighted building fronting on the square. Through its doorway

DISSOLVE TO:

44A. INT. AN INNER ROOM NIGHT

We start on the insert of a picture of Lincoln. Camera dollies back and over the shoulders of Juárez in a black frockcoat, seated at a desk, so we can read the address on an envelope that Juárez is opening with a paper knife. The envelope is addressed to

His Excellency:
Benito Juárez
President of the Republic of Mexico

As he takes the letter from the envelope the camera moves to:

44B. INSERT LETTER

It reads:

Dear Mr. President:

Permit me to express my deepest admiration for the courage and devotion with which you and your compatriots in the republic have defended the democratic principle.

God willing, our own civil war will soon be over; and when it is, I promise you that I shall do all in my power to aid you in your struggle.

Yours sincerely,
A. Lincoln[30]

44C. ANOTHER ANGLE JUÁREZ
Still shooting so that we do not see his face. After he has finished reading the letter, he puts it aside. Then he picks up a quill and starts writing on a large sheet of paper. The camera moves closer to the paper so that we see his hand write:

The Constitutional President of
the Republic, to the People of Mexico:

We dissolve to the same sheet of paper filled with the written text of the message, with Juárez's hand writing the last lines. The camera pulls back past Juárez and pans slowly over to a place near the desk, and we discover a Mexican peon, Juárez's servant, called Camilo. He is watching the man behind the desk, who nods to the peon. The latter shambles across to the door and opens it.

CUT TO:

44D. INT. ANTEROOM TEJADA, URADI, ESCOBEDO, PALACIO, REGULES, DÍAZ, CARBAJAL, AND NEGRONI
are in the scene. The peon indicates that they are to enter.

CUT TO:

45. THE INNER ROOM
The generals seen outside enter, led by the fiery young Porfirio Díaz. Without a word the Indian hands him the neatly written sheet of paper, and after a preliminary glance the soldier commences to read aloud, his voice controlled but passionate.

DÍAZ:

"The Constitutional President of the Republic, to the People of Mexico: Mexicans! The guilt of Napoleon III, whose lust for conquest has destroyed thousands of Mexicans; the guilt of those traitors here at home who would sell their birthright to foreigners for the privilege of exploiting their fellow countrymen; the guilt of all who have conspired to commit the gravest crime against civilization—which is the despoiling of the liberty of a free people—now embodies itself in the person of the usurper, Maximilian von Hapsburg.

"Let him who would come to our shores to rule over us as a tyrant know that the cause of democracy has not perished, and shall not perish. Let him know that to us the defense of democracy is an imperative duty, since it is the defense of our own honor, the dignity of our wives and children, the honor and dignity of all men.

"Let him know that the struggle of right against might shall never cease in Mexico until the last patriot lies with the thousands upon thousands who have already laid down their lives for truth, liberty, and justice.

"Done at Saltillo, this first day of May, 1864."

After reading the last words, the general looks at the Indian, his expression burning bright, hard, and determined.

CUT TO:

46. CLOSE-UP THE OTHER FACES
each reflecting the same fierce brightness.

CUT BACK TO:

47. TWO-SHOT
as Díaz hands back the document to the Indian, who picks up a quill.

CUT TO:

48. INSERT A BROWN HAND
signing: Benito Juárez

CUT TO:

49. CLOSE-UP BENITO JUÁREZ
immobile as a stone image, still seated at the desk.

DISSOLVE TO:

49A. (ALREADY SHOT)
The scene in which the plebiscite results are read off and Montares makes the remark that everything is ready for the reception of the new emperor of Mexico.

DISSOLVE TO:

50. MED. SHOT MAXIMILIAN AND CARLOTTA VON HAPSBURG
ascending the ramp of the quay to set first foot upon Mexican soil.[31] Below can be seen an admiral's barge which has brought them to shore, its double-banked crew standing in the thwarts with oars aloft at the salute. The anthem is sounding, and minute guns are booming over the scene. As the sovereigns approach the camera

PAN TO:

51. FULL SHOT THE EMBARCADERO AT VERACRUZ
situated at the foot of a wide, empty street, the intersection of which has been decorated with an arch of triumph topped by the imperial signet (a crown about the letter *M*). Near the arch the royal coach stands waiting. Buildings fronting on the quay are decorated with bunting, and upon their flat cornices are a row of hideous bird figures, spaced at regular intervals.

Massed units of French infantry present arms, their bands playing the Mexican anthem, their colors lowering to the ground in a royal salute. Señor Montares, silk hat in hand, stands slightly in advance of two other Mexicans, one of whom is a high cleric, the second (like Montares) in evening dress with a broad ribbon across his shirtfront. No other civilians are in view anywhere, but in rear of the three is a small group of officers in French uniforms, headed by Maréchal Bazaine.

CUT TO:

52. THREE-SHOT MONTARES, MAXIMILIAN, AND CARLOTTA

MONTARES:

At so momentous and long attended an instant in her history, the eager heart of Mexico is too full of pride and gratitude to speak more than the words, "Welcome, Your Imperial Majesties." (He bows to the midwaist and kisses their hands.)

MAXIMILIAN:

It is with a feeling of profound reverence, señor, that we set foot upon this soil, in the full consciousness of our obligation to it and to those who have entrusted their destinies to our hands.

53. GROUP SHOT

as the sovereigns arise and Montares continues his introductions.

MONTARES:

With Your Imperial Majesty's permission, the liberator of Mexico, Maréchal Achille Bazaine. (Bazaine salutes.)

MAXIMILIAN (seeing the Frenchman wishes to address him):

M'sieu le Maréchal . . .

BAZAINE:

Your Imperial Majesties, it is my privilege to convey the congratulations of the French Army of Occupation to you upon this historic occasion and to welcome you to Mexico.

MAXIMILIAN:

We are grateful to the Army of Occupation and to you personally, M'sieu le Maréchal. The emperor Napoleon spoke most flatteringly to us of your capabilities, not only as a soldier but in affairs of state as well.

As Montares leads a way to the waiting coach Carlotta's look travels over the scene.

CUT TO:

54. THE ARCH OF TRIUMPH
topped by the imperial signet. Upon its crown now rests an evil bird-figure similar to those which line the cornices of the buildings. Suddenly it moves.

CUT TO:

55. CLOSE SHOT GROUP CARLOTTA AND MAXIMILIAN IN FOREGROUND

CARLOTTA (grasping the emperor's arm in fright):
Oh! Max'l, it's alive!

The startled emperor follows her looks.

CUT TO:

56. CLOSE SHOT THE BIRD ON THE CROWN
A zopilote vulture[32] preening itself. Pan to show the lines of others on the buildings.

CUT BACK TO:

57. GROUP SHOT CARLOTTA, MAXIMILIAN, AND REGENCY COMMITTEE

MONTARES:
It is one of Your Majesty's most valuable servants. The vultures of Mexico are protected by law. They are the scavengers of its cities, consuming all garbage and keeping the streets clean . . .

58. MED. CLOSE SHOT THE ROYAL COACH
with a handsome Mexican officer in the brilliant uniform of the Emperatriz Regiment standing by its door.

MONTARES:
The commander of the escort, Colonel Miguel López, who is charged with Your Majesties' personal safety.

López salutes with bravura.

MAXIMILIAN (after a questioning look around):
You have a large command, Colonel. Is there a possibility that we may be attacked?

LÓPEZ (smiling as he glances toward the troops):
Not the slightest, sire. We only wish to secure Your Majesties' sacred persons against any intrusions.

CARLOTTA (smiling):
We shall feel very safe in your charge, Colonel López. (She gives him her hand to kiss, and he helps her into the royal coach. Maximilian follows.)

LÓPEZ (closing the door):
Your Majesties will travel over the exact route that Hernándo Cortés followed in his conquest of Mexico.[33]

The Regency Committee and Bazaine get into a second coach, while in the background members of the imperial suite can be glimpsed entering other conveyances. López mounts and gives the order "Adelante!" A bugle sounds, and, preceded by a cavalry escort, the royal coach commences to roll. Dolly with it through the arch of triumph into an empty, vulture-warded street, with soldiers spaced close against the buildings at regular intervals and only a few starving cur dogs in view. The clatter of horse hooves sounds over the scene.

CUT TO:

59. EXT. STREET
with Colonel López also in view, riding beside an open window of the coach.

MAXIMILIAN:
Colonel López, why are there no townspeople to greet us . . . ? Where is everyone . . . ? Why are the streets empty except for soldiers?

LÓPEZ:
Because of the plague, Your Majesty.

MAXIMILIAN:
What plague?

LÓPEZ:

Black plague, Your Majesty. There is an epidemic in the city and all public gatherings have been forbidden by law.

Maximilian nods and turns his look from López to the window on the other side of the coach.

CUT TO:

60. INSERT

The words Viva Juárez newly smeared in tar on the white wall of a passing building.

CUT BACK TO:

61. INT. COACH LÓPEZ AT WINDOW

CARLOTTA (who also has seen the inscription):

Colonel López, can we not go faster?

LÓPEZ (smiling):

I am afraid, Your Majesty, that we must travel at the pace of Mexico.

CUT TO:

62. INT. COACH CLOSE SHOT MAXIMILIAN AND CARLOTTA

as his firm hand closes over hers. Hold on them for a second or two, looking straight ahead and

DISSOLVE TO:

63. A MONTAGE OF MEXICO

Its mountains, jungles, pyramids, etc., illustrative of the sovereigns' progress toward the capital.

DISSOLVE TO:

64. INT. HEAVY COACH (PROCESS)

wending its way into steep, mountainous country. Maximilian and Carlotta are watching the tropical vegetation and the towering mountain ranges from a window.

MAXIMILIAN:

It is terrifying, this land—in its vastness, its wildness— Not to be measured by European standards of beauty— There the countryside, its streams and forests, are landscaped as it were—subdued by man—But here the land is master . . . not man.

CARLOTTA:

What are its people like, I wonder? Montares, López, and the others—they talk and act like Europeans, but what are they inside?[34]

MAXIMILIAN:

Since we set foot off the ship, I have felt myself surrounded by mystery—as though everything we looked at possessed some hidden meaning—not to be comprehended by the uninitiated.

CARLOTTA:

It has touched me too, Max'l . . . And it has made me apprehensive at having urged you so much toward this undertaking . . . Was it perhaps ambition for you that made me speak as I did . . . ? You must never let my opinions influence your own best judgment, dearest.

MAXIMILIAN (taking her hand):

I rely in your influence, Liebchen . . . You have a comprehension that lets you see into the heart of things . . . You were right in setting me on the road to my manifest destiny.

CARLOTTA (shivering slightly after a glance at the towering snow peaks on the skyline):

It is growing colder very quickly, Max'l. Let us have a rug.

Maximilian takes a robe from a corner of the opposite seat, and by so doing reveals an envelope on the upholstery.

CUT TO:

65. INSERT
of an envelope addressed to His Serene Highness, the Archduke Maximilian von Hapsburg of Austria.

CUT TO:

66. INT. CARRIAGE TWO-SHOT CARLOTTA AND MAXIMILIAN
as he reads the contents of the envelope aloud.

MAXIMILIAN:

"If Your Serene Highness is an honorable man, I tell you that you are the victim of a fraud which was designed to make you believe that the people of Mexico desired a monarch; and I tell you to leave Mexico and never return in the role of an emperor. But if Your Serene Highness is without honor, and yourself a party to this fraud, I commend you to your own conscience and the tremendous judgment of history. Benito Juárez."

They look at each other gravely with apprehension in their eyes.

CUT TO:

67. THE COACHMAN ON THE BOX
a distinctive peon type, handling whip and ribbons like an expert.

DISSOLVE TO:

68. MED. SHOT INT. ROOM IN A MEXICAN HOUSE AT SALTILLO[35]
Seated around a long table, piled with military maps, are several generals including Díaz, Escobedo, Carbajal, Palacio, Negroni, and Uradi. Juárez sits at the head of the table. They are all listening, with close attention, to the report of the coachman, whom we have previously seen as the one driving Maximilian's coach.

COACHMAN:

It was just after we left the pueblo of San Vincente and were going up into the mountains that they found the letter. Maximilian and Carlotta sat in troubled silence for a long time after they read it.

DÍAZ (after a pause):
Is his uniform very splendid?

The coachman slowly shakes his head, and it is obvious from his manner that he is, himself, impressed with Maximilian.

COACHMAN:
Yes, señor, he is a magnífico . . . tall, taller by a head than any of us, with blue eyes and a beard yellow like the silk of the corn. The Indians thought . . . many of them . . . that he was the fair god Quetzalcoatl come back again.[36]

URADI:
The blond god of the Aztec Indians, who promised to return someday, when he sailed away into the sunrise.

DÍAZ (heatedly):
They won't think him a god when he takes back their lands.

COACHMAN:
You should have seen their entrance into Mexico City. They were acclaimed, señores, even by many who hate the French.

DÍAZ (grimly):
We know . . .

CARBAJAL:
The blood must be let out of all that magnificence.

COACHMAN:
The servants in the palace say that four times every day Maximilian changes his clothes, down to his skin: once in the morning when he rides his horse; once when he sits with his ministers; once when he walks with Carlotta by the pool in the park; and once again before he eats dinner.

CARBAJAL:

They walk by the pool in the park, you say? Are they guarded when they walk there?

COACHMAN:

No, señor.

ESCOBEDO:

Well done, Manuel . . . go back now and find out whatever else you can.

COACHMAN (exits):

Adiós, señores.

CARBAJAL:

There are thickets around the pool . . . deep thickets, where a man with a knife could wait. (He makes a gesture of running his thumb along a blade.) Eh—señores?

JUÁREZ:

No, Carbajal, we are not assassins . . . nor are we, as Napoleon would have the world believe, a pack of savage bandits. A responsible government does not stab a man in the back. His crime must be judged according to the laws of the land. It is the Mexican people who will punish the man who calls himself their emperor.

URADI (expansively):

You are quite right, Señor Presidente; our cause has suffered enough, heaven knows, from the impression in Europe that none of us are persons of culture and refinement.

PALACIO:

I am less concerned about what Europe thinks of our social graces, Señor Uradi, than I am about the Indians believing Maximilian to be a god. Mexico was first conquered because its people believed a European to be a god.

JUÁREZ:

That is the inevitable course of tyranny, from Caesar to Napoleon. Tyrants always make their appearance in that guise, Palacio, because to exist they must, like gods, be the objects of the people's blind faith, a faith which enslaves rather than uplifts. And when a people is sufficiently weakened, only then does a despot unmask himself . . . but it is too late, for then the people are slaves. It is our task to strip the cloak of godliness from him and show him to the Mexican people for what he is—a tyrant.

PALACIO:

That may not be so easy, Don Benito.

JUÁREZ:

We must not lose courage . . . Buenos días, señores.

All exit with the usual "adiós, Señor Presidente, adiós, Don Benito," save Uradi, who remains behind, standing silent until the others have disappeared. Then he sits down across the desk from the Indian, who looks at him inquiringly.

URADI (frowning heavily):

Don Benito, what I must say to you, I can express only with the deepest pain and embarrassment. But, as you yourself would be the first to admit, the cause of liberty must come before everything else . . . even personal affection.

JUÁREZ:

Well . . . ?

URADI:

Those of us . . . who are close to you . . . are well aware of your wisdom . . . your humanity . . . your capacity for government. But in the eyes of the world . . . in the eyes of many Mexicans, you are—an Indian.

JUÁREZ:

Well . . . ?

URADI:

I assure you of my loyalty and devotion, Don Benito . . .

JUÁREZ:

Well . . . ?

URADI:

The influence of this Hapsburg . . . Are the forces combatting it best represented by the figure of one like yourself . . . an Indian? Does it not make our cause appear a racial struggle, instead of the struggle of a whole people?

JUÁREZ:

Well . . . ?

URADI:

Don Benito, I would sooner have my tongue cut out than say it . . . but I believe you should make room for another—yes, resign in favor of someone of European blood.

JUÁREZ:

You, as vice-presidente of the republic, would naturally be my successor . . .

URADI:

Whoever takes over the office will do so in name only . . . You would continue to be the real power . . . Your voice would command . . . Your will would be obeyed.

JUÁREZ:

Pure Spanish, are you not, Señor Uradi?

URADI:

There is not a drop of any other blood in my veins.

JUÁREZ:

There is much merit in what you say. Your concern is not unfounded. It was, perhaps, gross neglect on my part not to remind the oppressed element who elected me that because of my Indian blood I was unfit to reclaim for them their human heritage. But isn't it peculiar that a distressed and starving people do not think to ask whether the man elected as their choice is of good enough stock and breeding? It seems that in their anxiety to be freed from oppression and misery they overlooked that most important fact. It is true I'm a poor, ugly figure of an Indian indeed to be opposing one like him, one so magnificent that he is taken for a god by my despised and downtrodden brothers, but is not the struggle of any downtrodden element the struggle of the whole people? Would I not be betraying their trust in me were I to abandon them only because I am one of them?

DISSOLVE TO:

69. CLOSE SHOT MAXIMILIAN VON HAPSBURG DAY

mantled in his estate as emperor of Mexico, with the crown imperial and scepter on a taboret by his side (in the manner of the Winterhalter portrait which serves as a frontispiece to *Phantom Crown*, save that the mantle should be closed and the cape in view).

PULL BACK TO:

70. FULL SHOT THE ROBING ROOM AT CHAPULTEPEC PALACE[37] DAY

revealing that Maximilian is merely being fitted for his coronation robes. López is arranging the emperor's train. Various garments are carefully laid out on a table nearby. Footmen are in attendance, and a master tailor with two journeymen are also in evidence.

MAXIMILIAN:

It is understood then that the ermine border of the mantle must be increased to a width of eight inches, with miniver tails at intervals of six instead of twelve inches. (He smiles.) To distinguish me from an archduke, Colonel López.

LÓPEZ (rising):

Yes, Your Majesty . . . Your Majesty will forgive our ignorance of such refinements here in Mexico.

71. CLOSE-UP

somewhat as López removes the huge mantle with the aid of footmen, to reveal Maximilian in a long black coat and conventional trousers. The footmen fold up the mantle in the background and arrange the other garments for return to the wardrobe.

MAXIMILIAN (with a sigh of relief):

The ancient Aztec emperors were more fortunate than I am, Colonel . . . Their robes were of feathers . . .[38]

Dr. Basch, a little man of professional appearance, enters the scene with a medicine bottle and a vial on a silver salver.

BASCH:

It is twelve o'clock and time for Your Majesty's quinine.

MAXIMILIAN:

Dr. Basch! I wonder what the people who call me a tyrant would say if they had to live under you? (In the background, Colonel López can be seen leading off a parade of footmen bearing the robes, with the three tailors bringing up the rear.) I suppose there is no avoiding of it! (He drains the vial and makes a grimace.) Faugh . . .

BASCH (bowing to indicate his wanting to withdraw):

With Your Majesty's permission . . .

MAXIMILIAN (putting an arm over Basch's shoulder):
Not at all, Basch . . . ! For asserting your authority in so brutal a manner, you will talk to me while I daub at a canvas on the terrace. (Pan as the pair commence to exit together.) But first let us find Her Majesty. There is a slight change in the order of her household for the coronation ceremony which perhaps I should mention to her at once.

BASCH (a little concerned):
The empress is not in the palace at the present moment, Your Majesty.

MAXIMILIAN:
Indeed . . . where has she gone?

BASCH (shaking his head sadly):
Upon the vainest of pilgrimages, Your Majesty. The empress was told of the particular virtue attributed to the shrine of the Virgin at Verde, and insisted upon being taken there this morning.

DISSOLVE TO:

72. MED. SHOT EXT. SHRINE OF THE VIRGIN AT VERDE
It is a simple statue of the Madonna, with the Child in her arms, but set upon a mound, probably covering an ancient Aztec pyramid, as a flight of rough stone steps mount to the summit. Shooting midway up the mound and across the stairway toward the statue, twin files of women, all clad in black, pass the camera, climbing painfully upon their knees from step to step, and telling their beads as they go. Over the scene sounds the broken murmur of voices repeating Ave Marias in individual tempos. Hold the shot until a white-clad figure, side by side with a black-gowned peon woman, passes close by the lens.

CARLOTTA (blanching at the pain of bleeding knees, but telling her beads and reciting in unbroken rhythm):
Ave Maria, gratia plena, Dominus tecum, benedicta

tu in mulieribus et benedictus fructus ventris tui, Jesus . . . etc., etc. (Per Roman Catholic prayer book.)

73. CLOSE SHOT CARLOTTA BEFORE THE SHRINE SHOOTING UPWARD FROM HER ANGLE
to show a smile of compassion upon the Virgin's Indian face as she looks over the infant Jesus at the suppliant empress of Mexico below.

CARLOTTA (her arms around the feet of the Virgin; her eyes upon the Child; in desperate intensity):

Holy Mary, Mother of God, harken unto me, the least, the most humble of thy suppliants. Deny me not, I beseech thee, the pain and the agony which were thine. Deny me not, Most Blessed of Women, the joy and the ecstasy which thou knew. Endow me with a portion of thy sanctity and cause thy face to shine upon me, that through thy most compassionate intercession I may quicken and bear unto my spouse a son, even as thou did bear unto thy heavenly spouse, Our Lord and Savior Jesus Christ. Harken, I beseech thee, O Queen of Heaven, and here I vow unto thee for thy intercession a humble, grateful heart, a chapel domed in lapis lazuli, an altar of alabaster and thine image in the finest gold . . . to the glory of thy Holy Name.

Pull back to show the prostrate forms of black-clad women around Carlotta.

ALL:

Amen.

DISSOLVE TO:

74. CLOSE TWO-SHOT MAXIMILIAN AND DR. BASCH IN A CORNER OF THE TERRACE AT CHAPULTEPEC
The emperor is painting at an easel, with a palette on his thumb, while Basch is seated comfortably nearby.

MAXIMILIAN (lowering his brush with a sigh):

Samuel, old friend, sometimes I wonder if we have been wise in not telling her that she can never have a child.

BASCH:

Hope, Your Majesty—even the vainest of hopes—is a potent solace to a woman's heart. Crush that hope, and who can say what the consequences might be. No, Your Majesty, I do not regret that we have concealed the truth from her.

Maximilian nods and takes up his brush again. A liveried footman enters the scene.

FOOTMAN:

M'sieu le Maréchal Bazaine and Señor de Montares request an informal audience with Your Majesty.

MAXIMILIAN:

We shall receive them in our study.

DISSOLVE TO:

75. INT. MAXIMILIAN'S STUDY CHAPULTEPEC DAY

It is a wide, handsome room, with book-laden shelves. Maximilian is seated at a large writing table. On the wall behind him hangs a big map of Mexico. Bazaine and Montares have just made themselves at ease. The emperor is smoking a cigar and Bazaine a long-tubed cigarette.

MONTARES:

The maréchal and I wish to consult you with regard to certain details of the coronation ceremony . . . There is a question in my mind as to the seating of the foreign diplomats . . .

MAXIMILIAN:

Oh, there can be no great problem in that, Señor Montares. Diplomats take precedence according to their length of service at a court . . . without regard to rank or nationality. Let me see your plan . . .

CUT TO:

76. TWO-SHOT MAXIMILIAN AND MONTARES

MONTARES (unrolling and laying down a sheet of paper before the emperor):

Here it is, Your Majesty.

MAXIMILIAN (looks up after a moment's inspection):

I find no provision here for a minister from the United States?

MONTARES:

There is no United States minister in Mexico City, Your Majesty!

MAXIMILIAN (somewhat startled):

Indeed! And how do you account for that, señor?

MONTARES (frowning; and after a pause):

The impression is that the United States still recognize the old republic, Your Majesty. Of course, a democracy has to save its face under such circumstances; but it will inevitably come around in due course, now that the empire has been recognized by the other great powers.[39]

MAXIMILIAN (raising his eyebrows):

You say that they still recognize the old republic . . . Do you mean that they look upon Benito Juárez as the head of a legal Mexican government?

MONTARES:

Whether they actually have an envoy accredited to Juárez, I cannot say.

77. THREE-SHOT

MAXIMILIAN (turning to the Frenchman):

Maréchal Bazaine, how many men are with Benito Juárez?

BAZAINE:

Well, about twenty-five thousand men in his northern armies—

MAXIMILIAN:

Twenty-five thousand men!

BAZAINE:

Yes, sire—and in the south about twelve thousand.

MAXIMILIAN (after a long pause):

I had no idea—no idea. (He rises and walks the length of the room.) Maréchal Bazaine, my understanding was that the country had been completely pacified . . . that no such things as organized republican government and organized republican resistance continued to exist . . . These revelations come as a grave shock to me. (He continues to walk up and down.)

MONTARES:

The situation is far from being as serious as it must sound to Your Majesty.

BAZAINE (heavily reassuring):

Of course not, Your Majesty. The republican army is an undisciplined rabble—poorly armed—without leadership—

MAXIMILIAN (stopping):

I am no militarist, Maréchal . . . I did not come here to conquer but to rule—peacefully! To that end let us enter into negotiations with Benito Juárez immediately.

BAZAINE:

Negotiations! Your Imperial Majesty might as well try to come to terms with a wild animal in the jungle . . . The whip, the bullet, and the bayonet is the only language his kind understand.

MAXIMILIAN (producing a letter):

I discovered this letter from the Indian in my coach on the way from Veracruz. (He hands it to the maréchal.) It is difficult to associate its words with the savage you describe. (As Bazaine looks up from the script with a frown.) And what does he imply when he says I am the victim of a fraud?

BAZAINE (with a shrug):
I suppose he has reference to the plebiscite . . . It is the usual custom here in Mexico for the loser of an election to make accusations of fraud and coercion—

MAXIMILIAN (interrupting):
In the face of a majority of ninety-nine percent!

MONTARES:
There is no limit to his falsehoods . . . to his audacity.

MAXIMILIAN:
And you insist, Maréchal Bazaine, that to try to negotiate with him would be hopeless?

BAZAINE:
Oh, I tried it myself when I first came here. I sent messenger after messenger to Benito Juárez—till I discovered that they were being shot, one after the other, as fast as they arrived . . .

MAXIMILIAN (in a shocked tone):
Incredible . . .

BAZAINE (simulating outrage):
You have no idea what Juárez is, Your Majesty—a beast . . . a bloodthirsty, ruthless beast . . . Yes, Your Majesty, the whip, the bullet, and the bayonet . . .

MAXIMILIAN:
What is to be done, Maréchal . . . ? After all, you've been here for two years without being able to subdue Juárez and his followers.[40]

BAZAINE:

Your Majesty need not trouble his mind about Benito Juárez any longer. The emperor Napoleon has reinforced me to fifty thousand men, with complete munitions for a final offensive which I am now ready to launch on all fronts. Within thirty days the Indian will be dead, captured, or driven out of the country. I guarantee it! (He picks up and cracks a riding crop against his boot.)

DISSOLVE TO:

78. A MONTAGE OF BAZAINE'S CAMPAIGN
against the republican armies, designed to reveal the superb equipment and mechanical precision of the French divisions, the corresponding deficiencies of materiel and discipline in the republican ranks, and finally an encounter in which the sacrifice and courage of the *Juaristas* are of no avail against the paralysing shock and envelopment of the Napoleonic war machine.

DISSOLVE TO:

78A. MED. SHOT INT. OFFICE OF BENITO JUÁREZ SALTILLO DAY
The room is the same as in the preceding Juárez scene, with the picture of Lincoln in evidence on a wall. Juárez is seated at his desk, poring over a large military map spread out upon it. It is evident that he is struggling with an extremely difficult problem. From time to time he inserts and removes various colored pins at different points on the map.

Abruptly, with a gesture of mingled bafflement and fatigue, he brushes the pins aside, gets up from the desk, and, after a few aimless paces, stands looking out the window as if expecting someone.

At this point, Camilo enters carrying a bowl of some sort of stew. As he advances toward the desk he speaks.

CAMILO:

Don Benito . . . time to eat . . . (Places bowl on desk.) It is not much, but there is so little left.

Juárez, preoccupied at the window, does not answer.

CAMILO (pleadingly):

Don Benito . . . *eat*.

There is a sudden murmur of voices outside, followed by a timid knock at the door. Juárez looks around expectantly. Camilo goes to the door, exits, closing door after him. As Juárez stands there, looking and listening intently, we hear Camilo's voice raised querulously.

CAMILO:

No, no . . . Don Benito is busy . . . He is eating now. (The door opens and Camilo comes back into the room exclaiming irately to Juárez.) Such donkeys! They think you have time to talk to every farmer that comes to market . . .

JUÁREZ (on the alert):

Farmers? Let them come in.

CAMILO:

But . . . but . . .

JUÁREZ:

Let them come in . . .

Camilo grumblingly shuffles to the door, opens it, and admits a group of Indian peons. They file in timidly, each bearing some form of produce—chickens, baskets of vegetables, melons, cheese, etc. Juárez stands a little to one side of his desk and appears to be scanning their faces intently. An old jefe steps forward from the group and speaks.

JEFE:

I've come a long way to see you in the name of my people. They are grateful to you. They send you this.

He places a basket of vegetables on the desk. Another peon steps forward, extending some fruit.

PEON:

Our harvest was poor, but this is from our hearts.

In quick succession, the various peons step forward and place their gifts upon the desk, saying, "This is from us," "Take mine, too," "For your good health, Don Benito," "May you live long, and drive out the enemy."

After three or four have presented their offerings, one of the group steps forward with a large oyster or mussel and, approaching more closely than the others, says:

FIRST SPY (in a significant tone):

This is from Michoacán, Señor Presidente. It is said by our fathers that a pearl of wisdom is often found in such.

Juárez throws him a sharp glance, takes the shellfish with a nod of thanks, and sets it to one side. One or two other peons follow with their presents and then another peon steps forward bearing a cactus plant.

SECOND SPY:

I am from Tamaulipas, Señor Presidente. They say that in our cactus lies hidden the seeds of truth.

Juárez looks sharply at this peon also and places the cactus alongside the shellfish.

All the gifts having been presented, the peons have all stepped back and formed a little group, including the two peon spies, who are superficially indistinguishable from the others. They wait expectantly for Juárez to speak.

Juárez slowly surveys the piled-up gifts and the eager faces of the peons. Underneath his stolid features there is a ripple of profound emotion. After a pause, he speaks:

JUÁREZ:

Hermanos . . . amigos . . . your devotion brings me comfort and gives me great strength. Tell your people that I will not forget that I am their son . . . Adiós, compañeros.

The peons leave, murmuring various forms of good-bye. Camilo ushers them out. As soon as he is alone, Juárez turns to the shellfish and the cactus; he carefully pries open the shellfish and finds a rolled-up message inside. As he spreads it out on the desk we

CUT TO:

78B. INSERT THE MESSAGE
which reads:

> Uruapan, 100 men . . . Zamora, 150 . . . Cherán, 70 . . . Juaja, 50 . . . My sector of this state now organized. Can act upon receiving funds for powder and guns. R.[41]

CUT BACK TO:

78C. JUÁREZ
He swiftly splits the cactus fruit with a knife. Tucked away in its hollowed-out core is another slip of paper. As Juárez is reading this second slip, Camilo enters, pushing a diffident Pepe before him. He motions Pepe close to the desk. The boy stands there, smiling shyly.

CAMILO:
Don Benito . . .

Juárez looks up, sees the boy, then looks at Camilo inquiringly.

JUÁREZ (with a faint smile):
Who is this boy . . . ? What does he want?

PEPE:
I am Pepe.

CAMILO (beaming):
He is Pepe!

JUÁREZ (puzzled):
Pepe?

CAMILO (proudly, with a broad grin):
Yes . . . my son! He has a message for you.

PEPE (with sudden assurance):
From Señor Perez. He says everyone in Oaxaca will be ready to fight again as soon as you send them the guns and bullets.

JUÁREZ (appreciatively):
You are a brave boy, Pepe.

PEPE (cuts in):
And a good shepherd, too.

JUÁREZ (fraternally):
Was it a good spring for the grass in Oaxaca this year?

PEPE (seriously):
No, it was very bad, Don Benito. I had to take my sheep to the high country, and a timber wolf killed three ewes.

JUÁREZ:
What did you do?

PEPE:
I set my dogs on him . . . but at first they didn't know the right way to fight him; then they learned the right way.

JUÁREZ (his attention begins to wander a little as his eyes are drawn back to the messages and the map):
And what was the right way, Pepe?

PEPE (with animated gestures):
They found out he would turn to chase whichever of them bit him. So they made a big ring around him. When he chased Malo, Pinta came down and bit his hind legs. When he turned after Pinta, Chico ran in and bit his flank. When he turned after Chico, Fea came up and bit his other flank. And when he turned after Fea, Malo rushed in and it began all over again . . . Then, when he was too tired and too torn to run anymore, they all closed in and killed him.[42]

During all this, Juárez at first looked up at the boy, from time to time, nodding encouragingly, but as the recital progressed, he became more and more absorbed in the map, and began to quickly place the colored pins in a series of points forming an irregular circle. As Pepe says "they all closed in and killed him" Juárez vigorously thrusts the last pin in the center of the circle and looks up at the boy.

JUÁREZ:

> Yes, Pepe . . . *that* is the right way to fight the wolf.

At this point there is an imperative knock on the door, and before Camilo can answer, a dust-covered horseman strides in.

MESSENGER:

> Señor Presidente! Monterrey has fallen! We must abandon Saltillo and retreat to the west. General Escobedo wishes you to leave at once, before the road is blocked by troops.

Juárez receives this news as if he had been prepared for it. After a slight pause, he dismisses the messenger with a silent gesture and turns to Camilo.

JUÁREZ:

> Camilo, take nothing but my papers . . . (To Pepe.) Come, Pepe, put this valise in the carriage. (He picks up a portfolio and hurries to the door. At the door he stops, turns around, and points to the picture of Lincoln.) And Camilo . . . the picture . . .

CAMILO:

> The gringo?

JUÁREZ:

> Yes, Camilo, the gringo . . . (He goes out.)

Camilo grabs the papers, etc., from the desk, runs over to the wall, takes down the picture, then runs back to the desk for more papers, when he suddenly notices the untouched bowl of food. With a muttered expletive, he jams the picture and the papers under one arm, grabs the bowl of food in the other hand, and dashes to the door with an expression of grim determination upon his face.

78D. EXT. JUÁREZ'S OFFICE SALTILLO DAY

As Camilo emerges from the house he finds Juárez inside the carriage, with Pepe piling in various boxes, books, files, etc., at Juárez's direction. Camilo runs over to the carriage, thrusts the bowl of food under Juárez's nose, and in a voice at once fierce and pleading, says:

CAMILO:

Eat!

Juárez looks up at Camilo with a startled expression which quickly turns to one of mingled love and gratitude. Camilo can almost feel tears in his eyes, although he does not cry. He meekly takes the bowl in his hands. With a grunt of satisfaction, Camilo swings away, jumps up to the driver's seat, whips up the horses, and they are off, Pepe waving them goodbye.

CUT TO:

78E. INT. CARRIAGE JUÁREZ

amid the overwhelming clutter of packages, valises, books, etc., jouncing about him, soberly eating from the bowl in his hand.

DISSOLVE TO:

79. INT. OF A LARGE TENT OR MARQUEE

which is the field headquarters of Mariano Escobedo, commander in chief of the *Juarista* northern army. He is seated at a table working over maps and order forms, while Uradi paces the floor. In the background, kit and bedding are being packed by a servant, who leaves it rolled and strapped as he exits. Gallopers, runners, and orderlies enter and exit periodically throughout the scene, to deliver or carry away dispatches. Through the open tent flap can be seen other tents of the army command, a guard post, etc. There is the sound of hoofbeats as Porfirio Díaz reins up at the entrance and dismounts. Negroni is present among the generals.

DÍAZ (entering):
Is it true that Monterrey has fallen?

ESCOBEDO:
Yes . . . Rivera's whole command has been wiped out. The French caught his counterattack in a cross fire and mowed it down like wheat.

URADI:
They're not an army but a machine . . . a war machine.

ESCOBEDO:
Our only line of retreat is now to the west . . . through the pass at Encantada.

URADI:
Pour two routed divisions through that bottleneck! If Bazaine's cavalry can reach it, we're trapped like rats.

ESCOBEDO:
All we can do is pray our rear guard holds. (He picks up an order blank.) I'll detach another battalion to support it. (He writes and hands the order to a runner.)

URADI:
Compañeros, what difference does it make if we get through the pass or not? The hour has come when we must face the truth or perish . . . We are hopelessly defeated. Are more and more lives—our own included—to be sacrificed for a dead cause; or shall we act now with wisdom instead of brute courage?

ESCOBEDO:

What do you mean, Señor Uradi?

URADI:

I mean that we should ask Bazaine for an armistice and come to terms with the empire.

The others look at him resentfully but troubled.

DÍAZ (grimly):

That is for Señor Juárez to say.

URADI:

Don Benito is miles away . . . safe and secure. (At these words, unseen to all save the audience, the shadow of a little man in a top hat appears on the wall of the tent.) Does he expect us to resist two French corps with a handful of broken battalions . . . ? I saw it coming long ago— (He turns startled as Juárez's voice comes over scene.)

JUÁREZ'S VOICE:

Buenos días, señores . . .

Pan to the doorway, where Benito Juárez is standing in his black frock coat and top hat, with an umbrella under his arm and a briefcase in his hand. Draw back to the full scene as he comes forward toward Uradi (and the camera) to stand before him with unblinking eyes.

DÍAZ:

Señor Juárez!

ESCOBEDO:

We are lost unless we can retreat through the pass at Encantada!

URADI:

And when we get through it—if we get through it—what then?

JUÁREZ:

Then we shall begin all over again . . . But we will fight no more pitched battles with the French. We shall stop fighting Bazaine *his* way and make him fight *our* way. The army will be disbanded. Officers and men will scatter and return to their own states, lie low, but keep in touch with one another, until they receive orders from me. Where the government will be, I do not know—a week here, a day there. The Capitol will be on wheels . . . my carriage. Doubtless it will be forced further and further back . . . even to the border of the United States. But it will never cross the border. For, as long as a constitutional government remains on Mexican soil, the Republic of Mexico continues to exist.

There is a sound of faraway cannon in the ensuing silence. Escobedo and Díaz suddenly start, exchange alarmed glances, and make for the door.

ESCOBEDO:

Saints of heaven! French gunfire—from the west!

To the end of the scene the sound of the firing increases progressively, but must never seem very near at hand.

DÍAZ:

That means that Bazaine is coming by the Avalos road to cut us off from the pass.

A bugle shrills a call and is answered by a dozen others. There is a clatter outside the tent. Escobedo returns to the table and, with Díaz looking over his shoulder, studies a staff map. Díaz picks up his gauntlets, hat, and quirt.

ESCOBEDO:

What are you going to do?

DÍAZ:

Attack the French! Delay them until the rest of our army can get through the pass. (Crosses to the president.) Adiós, Señor Juárez . . .

The Indian stands looking at Díaz for a long time. Then, after a quick abrazo (the Mexico "elbow embrace"):

JUÁREZ:

Adiós, Porfirio . . .

DISSOLVE TO:

79A. A FRENCH PATROL ON THE BATTLEFIELD AFTER THE FIGHT NIGHT

Hearing the groans of a wounded man, they seek for the sufferer and find him.

SOLDIER:

It's an officer.

A CORPORAL (as he turns the wounded man over):

A general!

The camera moves in to a close-up of the wounded man. It is Porfirio Díaz.

DISSOLVE TO:

80. COUNCIL CHAMBER IN THE PALACE OF CHAPULTEPEC

during a session of the Imperial Council. At a long table are Maximilian, the ministers Montares, de León, del Valle, Salas, and others, seated before their official portfolios; also Mejía and Miramón, listening to a report of the recent campaigns by Maréchal Bazaine.

BAZAINE:

. . . In other words, Imperial Majesty, all organized republican resistance has ceased to exist; General Porfirio Díaz is a prisoner in our hands, and Benito Juárez is either a fugitive in the deserts of Chihuahua or he has crossed the border into the United States.

MAXIMILIAN:

We are unqualifiedly grateful to you, M'sieu le Maréchal, and to the soldiers of France who have inaugurated this era of peace.

BAZAINE (rising):

My humble thanks, Your Imperial Majesty. (He assumes his kepi and salutes.) With Your Majesty's permission . . .

Maximilian bows a *congé* and the Frenchman exits.

MAXIMILIAN:

We are also grateful to the leaders of our loyal Mexican brigades who participated in the campaign. It is our wish that General Miguel Miramón shall become minister of war, and that General Tomás Mejía shall take rank as commander in chief of the Imperial Mexican Army.

At the latter pronouncement there is a near gasp from the ministers, who glance at one another in shocked amazement. An expression of intense pride and gratitude on the soldier's face dies away as he looks around him. Maximilian is the last to be conscious of the contretemps, but by this time Mejía is on his feet to forestall it.

MEJÍA:

It is too great an honor, Imperial Majesty . . . I cannot accept—being an Indian, I am unworthy.

MAXIMILIAN:

What has your race to do with your fitness to command, General Mejía?

MEJÍA (in utter embarrassment):

Everything, Imperial Majesty . . .

MAXIMILIAN:

Since you are of noble Aztec stock, no doubt your heritage of blood is the most ancient in this room . . . It is our will that you assume the post to which you have been raised, and it is our trust that you will do it great honor . . .

MONTARES:

And now, Your Imperial Majesty—more immediate business . . . (The members of the council bend forward as the prime minister picks up the formal instrument which has been before him since the early part of the session.) May I present for your signature the most pressing of all enactments . . . (He brings the instrument to the emperor in person.)

MAXIMILIAN (reading):

"An act restoring to the legal owners certain lands . . ." What does this refer to, Señor Montares?

MONTARES:

Those properties which were confiscated from their legal owners by Benito Juárez.

MAXIMILIAN:

Into whose hands did these lands pass?

MONTARES:

The hands of a million or more peons, Imperial Majesty.

MAXIMILIAN:

Did Benito Juárez divide the land amongst them?

MONTARES:

That is what it amounted to, Your Imperial Majesty. Actually, the lands were put up at auction.

MAXIMILIAN:

And who received the money paid in at these auctions?

MONTARES:

Why, the owners, sire. (Sensing Maximilian's trend of thought.) But what ridiculous sums . . . Nothing like the true worth.

MAXIMILIAN:

How much land was involved in these transactions, señores?

A MINISTER (indignantly):

About eighty percent of the arable land of all Mexico. That is what we were robbed of by Benito Juárez!

MAXIMILIAN:

And how many individual owners were concerned?

SAME MINISTER:

Eighty-five, Imperial Majesty . . . that is, eighty-five estates.

DE LEÓN:

The estates of the oldest and noblest families in Mexico. Their lands were grants of conquest and colonization from Your Majesty's own ancestors, the Hapsburg kings of Spain.

MAXIMILIAN (setting the instrument aside after a period of thought):

Señores, inasmuch as monies were paid and received at public auction, it would seem as if there were at least a semblance of legality in what took place . . . We cannot set our hand lightly to an instrument which might well be against the best interest of a vast majority of our subjects.

There is an immediate stir of blank astonishment among the members of the council, all of whom look questioningly toward Montares.

A MINISTER:

But—Your Majesty . . .

ANOTHER MINISTER:

The sanctity of vested rights—

MAXIMILIAN:

What of the peons . . . who would be without if the lands were to be taken away from them . . . ?

A MINISTER:

What if they are without land . . . ? They were without it for three hundred years—before Benito Juárez.

MAXIMILIAN:

Señores, when the vested rights of individuals conflict with the welfare of a nation, then the welfare of the nation must prevail.

MINISTER:

But those are the very words of Benito Juárez!

MONTARES (seeing it is now or never):

Your Imperial Majesty, the abrogation of these sales is an inflexible demand of the Conservative Party . . . the party which put you on the throne . . .

There is an almost snarled chorus of assent from the ministers.

MAXIMILIAN (very much the Hapsburg):

Señor Montares . . . the name of one responsible to a political party is politician, not emperor . . .

MONTARES:

It would cause us the deepest regret to resign from His Majesty's council at this early date in His Majesty's reign . . .

The others approve audibly.

MAXIMILIAN:

Your resignations are accepted, señores . . . We permit no one to infringe upon our prerogative to protect the best interests of the great majority of subjects.

At this calling of their bluff, the ministers are shocked into silence and turn blank faces on one another.

MONTARES (ironically):

"The great majority of His Majesty's subjects . . ." In returning my portfolio to Your Imperial Majesty . . . (he turns it face downward on the table) may I express the hope that he may be able to rely upon that same majority of his subjects in his hour of need.

The remaining ministers (within the camera's angle) likewise turn their portfolios face down, rise to their feet, and bow in unison.

MAXIMILIAN:

You have our leave to go, señores.

As they leave the scene draw back to show Mejía and Miramón (who have come up while masked by the camera) standing left and right of the emperor in the composition they are destined to assume on the Hill of the Bells.

MAXIMILIAN (seeing them; repeats):

You have our leave to go.

MEJÍA AND MIRAMÓN:

We are Your Majesty's servants.

MAXIMILIAN:

I am very grateful to you, gentlemen.

FADE OUT

FADE IN

81. CLOSE SHOT A WOODEN SIGN ON THE WALL OF A BUILDING

Against the background of a crudely painted facsimile of a foaming beer glass, the sign reads:

TEXAS JACK'S

The Best Beer in Brownsville

DISSOLVE TO:

82. CLOSE SHOT THREE BEER GLASSES ON A WOODEN TABLE
As the camera starts to move back we hear a man's voice saying:

MAN'S VOICE:
Frankly, señor, it seems the Conservative Party has made a great mistake in bringing Maximilian von Hapsburg to Mexico.

As the camera continues back we see Montares sitting at a table in the back room of a honky-tonky beer saloon of the period. Sitting next to him, puffing on a cigar, is Le Marc, a suave Creole. Montares continues talking across the table to a man sitting opposite him, whose face we do not see because camera is shooting over his shoulder.

MONTARES (continuing):
We took it for granted he would restore our lands. By refusing to do so, he has forfeited all claim to our loyalty.

The man to whom Montares has been talking nods in agreement.

MAN:
Naturally.

MONTARES:
The form of government is of no consequence to us. Our land is the thing. We would cheerfully live under any government which would return it to us.

MAN:
Even a republican government?

CUT TO:

83. ANOTHER ANGLE MONTARES AND THE MAN
We see that it is Uradi.

MONTARES (nodding slowly):
Even a republican government.

URADI:

Juárez will never change his attitude on the land question.

LE MARC:

And do you think his attitude right?

URADI (warily):

Well—not entirely. I have always felt his program a little—revolutionary.

There is a pause as Montares exchanges looks with Le Marc. Then, sipping his beer, Montares questions Uradi:

MONTARES (as if he didn't know):

Juárez's term of office expires soon, does it not, Señor Uradi?

URADI:

Not for some months.

MONTARES (his eyes on him):

And what if at that time it is impossible to hold a presidential election?

URADI (returning his gaze):

The Constitution then provides that the vice-president shall automatically succeed the president in office.

MONTARES:

So?

LE MARC (with a little smile):

An interesting provision, is it not, Señor Vice-Presidente?

URADI (shrugging a shoulder):

Perhaps . . . if there were any chance of the republic surviving till it took effect . . . (With a gesture.) But there is none . . . We have men, but no munitions . . . or money for munitions.

MONTARES (in cynical expansiveness):
Politics can indeed make strange bedfellows, señor . . . How incredible that it behooves us Conservatives to provide Benito Juárez with the funds for his struggle . . .

He sips daintily from his glass as Uradi stares at him.[43]

DISSOLVE TO:

84. LONG SHOT EXT. A ROAD
winding through sheer rocky cliffs in a deserted and lonely ridge of mountains. We see a man on horseback galloping along the narrow road.

DISSOLVE TO:

85. CLOSER SHOT THE ROAD
A rocky glen, overgrown with cactus and brush, opens on one side of the road. A weather-beaten, dilapidated shrine marks the intersection of the road with the entrance into the glen. The horseman comes down the road and turns into the glen.

CUT TO:

86. MED. SHOT THE GLEN
Grouped near their tethered horses are Escobedo, with several members of his staff, and Uradi. As the horseman comes into the scene and reins up we see that it is Carbajal.

CARBAJAL (greeting the group):
Compañeros!

They wave in greeting to him.

CUT TO:

87. CLOSER SHOT THE GROUP
Carbajal alights from his horse and inquires of Escobedo:

CARBAJAL:
Has he not come yet?

ESCOBEDO:

He should be here soon. The rains have made the back roads difficult. (Then a little wearily.) How are things in Nuevo León?

CARBAJAL (grimly shaking his head):

Bad, Mariano! There are many valientes but few rifles—and no bullets. The men are losing heart.

URADI:

They must be patient.

The group turns to look as in the background Juárez's mud-spattered carriage, with Juan on the box, drives into the glen and stops near them.

CUT TO:

88. CLOSER SHOT AT CARRIAGE

Juárez, worn and travel stained, gets out of the carriage and greets the group:

JUÁREZ:

Señores . . . (Then noticing Tejada's absence.) Has Señor Tejada not arrived from El Paso . . . ? He should have important news for us from Washington, now that the Civil War is ended . . .

ESCOBEDO:

No, Don Benito . . . he has not arrived . . . (Then, reluctant to tell him.) But there is news from Washington—

JUÁREZ:

Yes . . . ?

ESCOBEDO:

Abraham Lincoln is dead.

Juárez sags visibly. Carbajal is stunned.

JUÁREZ:

Lincoln—?

ESCOBEDO:

He was shot by an assassin and died the next day.

JUÁREZ (trying to control his shock; to Escobedo, after getting a grip on himself again):

General Escobedo—all flags of the republic will be flown at half-mast—all officers and members of the government will wear black armbands to mourn the loss of a friend.

CARBAJAL (despairing):

With him died our last hope of aid from his government. (He crosses away from the group.)

URADI:

Compañeros . . . help will come. We have lived through darker days. Don Benito will get munitions—somewhere—

Juárez and the others, a little surprised at Uradi's unusual optimism, turn to look inquiringly at him.

CARBAJAL:

If Uradi can still hope, then indeed all is not lost.[44]

CUT TO:

89. WIDER ANGLE

A carriage drives into the glen and stops near the group. They watch as Tejada gets out with Le Marc and crosses with him to Juárez and the others, who stare curiously at the stranger. At no time during the scene does Uradi or Le Marc give any indication that they have met before.

TEJADA:

Don Benito, may I present Señor Phillipe Le Marc of New Orleans . . .

Juárez extends his hand to Le Marc, who takes it.

JUÁREZ:

Our sympathy goes out to you and your countrymen in the loss of your great president.

LE MARC:

Thank you, Your Excellency.

TEJADA:

Señor Le Marc found me in El Paso. He has a message of such importance that I thought it necessary to bring him here.

LE MARC:

Señor Presidente—the Society of the Friends of Mexican Democracy—a society of Americans who have watched with warm admiration your splendid struggle for democracy—send you this memorial of their sympathies— (he hands the puzzled Juárez a document, which he takes from a small briefcase) and this draft for two hundred thousand pesos to be used at the discretion of the President of the Republic of Mexico. (He hands Juárez the check.)

JUÁREZ (a little incredulous as he takes it):

Two hundred thousand pesos?!

LE MARC (smiling):

More will follow from the new groups we are organizing all over the United States.

JUÁREZ:

Señor Le Marc, will you convey to your society the grateful thanks of the Mexican nation . . . Tell them we will never forget the help they have offered us in the hour of our necessity.

LE MARC:

I shall, Señor Presidente.

JUÁREZ (crossing with Le Marc and Tejada toward the carriage):

I am sorry I cannot accompany you to the border. Señor Tejada will see to your comfort.

LE MARC:

He already has—very considerably.

JUÁREZ (extending his hand):

Goodbye, Señor Le Marc.

LE MARC (taking it):

Goodbye, Your Excellency. I am certain when we meet again it will be in Mexico City.

JUÁREZ:

Thank you, señor.

Le Marc gets into the carriage, followed by Tejada.

CUT TO:

90. WIDER ANGLE

The group watches as the carriage drives out of the glen.

CUT TO:

91. MED. CLOSE SHOT JUÁREZ AND GROUP

Uradi watches Juárez as he stands, preoccupied, fingering the check.

URADI (with a forced smile):

You see, Don Benito? It is always darkest before dawn.

JUÁREZ:

I did not know that prophecy was one of your accomplishments, Señor Uradi!

URADI (laughing it off):

I am afraid not, Don Benito. It was just a feeling I had that help would come to us—from somewhere—

CARBAJAL (enthusiastically):

Two hundred thousand pesos! Now our guerrilla campaign can begin!

DISSOLVE TO:

92. OMITTED

93. CLOSE SHOT AN ARCHWAY

bearing the words Presidio de Zamora. Pan down to French sentries at the entrance of a barracks courtyard.[45]

PAN AROUND TO:

94. MED. LONG SHOT THE PLAZA OF A SMALL TOWN

About the square are many stalls for the sale of flowers, fruit, hats, pottery, pulque, etc. The vendors lounge and chatter over their wares in the warm afternoon sunshine. A wagon, loaded high with sheaves of sugar cane and hauled by two oxen, rumbles into the scene. The wagoner walks alongside his oxen, singing lustily "The Song of the Sugar Cane Vendor." (If there is no such song it ought to be written.)

CUT TO:

95. CLOSER SHOT THE WAGONER

although in peon costume, is recognizable as Carbajal. As he passes the French sentries he stops and tries to sell them some stalks of cane.

CARBAJAL:

Sugar cane, amigos . . . sugar cane . . . (The sentries are not interested. Carbajal, taking the stump of a cigar from his pocket, begs of one of the sentries.) Could the señor spare a match?

The sentry indifferently gives him a match. Carbajal lights his cigar. Then, resuming his song, he turns the wagon into the plaza, so that its tailboard is directly opposite the entrance to the barracks courtyard.

96. MED. CLOSE SHOT A SECTION OF THE STALLS IN THE PLAZA

where the word is being passed excitedly from mouth to mouth: "The cane has come, compañeros!"

CUT TO:

97. MED. CLOSE SHOT CARBAJAL

at the dropped tailboard of the wagon. In full view of the guards, he apparently commences to fuss with his cigar, but instead uses it to light the fuse of a crude grenade concealed under his coat. Draw back to a full shot of the wagon as he turns and throws the bomb at the French sentries.

CUT TO:

98. CLOSER SHOT THE WAGON
with the roar of the explosion over the scene. The sheaves of sugar cane are flung out on frames which supported them, to uncover a small gun being put into action by two men.

CUT TO:

99. MED. CLOSE SHOT THE STALLS IN THE PLAZA
From under the piles of fruits and vegetables we see the men snatch revolvers, rifles, machetes, etc., and run out of scene.

CUT TO:

100. MED. CLOSE SHOT COURTYARD OF THE BARRACKS
with the garrison rushing out from their quarters.

CUT TO:

101. WIDER ANGLE THE GUN
firing a charge of shrapnel into the packed Frenchmen. Led by Carbajal, a rush of market peons swarms past the camera and storms into the barracks.

DISSOLVE TO:

102. FULL SHOT
The flaming barracks and the empty plaza.

DISSOLVE TO:

103. MAXIMILIAN'S STUDY CHAPULTEPEC NIGHT
The emperor is in the midst of an interview with a choleric Maréchal Bazaine. As in the previous study scene, a large wall map of Mexico is prominent behind Maximilian's desk. Dupont is also present.

DUPONT:

. . . A peaceful enough country town on the surface; the plaza no quieter or no noisier than usual; everything the same as any other weekday . . . Suddenly an inferno breaks loose, and the garrison at Salinas . . . or Zamora . . . or Santiago . . . or fifty other places is wiped out. Supports arrive to find a deserted town and nobody for miles around who knows anything about what happened.

MAXIMILIAN:

These outbreaks—are they local revolutions, or is Benito Juárez behind them?

DUPONT:

Undoubtedly Juárez is behind them. Look at the map . . . The locations of the outbreaks and the order in which they occur show beyond question that they are all part of a devilish plan.

MAXIMILIAN (who has arisen and commenced to walk up and down, having ceased to listen before the end of Bazaine's speech):

So Juárez is not . . . finished. (Bazaine scowls and drums his fingers on the table.) What measures have you in mind, Maréchal?

BAZAINE:

Repressive ones, Your Majesty . . . We are no longer opposed by legitimate forces, but by an enemy masquerading as peaceful citizens. By treachery! It must be ground out . . . mercilessly.

Bazaine produces a document and tenders it to Maximilian. As the emperor reads it, an expression of incredulity on his face.

INSERT OF BLACK DECREE
irised down to the following passage: Anybody caught carrying arms will be shot within twenty-four hours.

MAXIMILIAN:

Do you want my signature to this?

BAZAINE:

Yes, Imperial Majesty.

Maximilian continues to read the document. Unconsciously his hand travels to his throat. Once he looks at Bazaine, as if for a spoken affirmation of the words he sees. Then his eyes go back to the document.

BAZAINE:

Your Majesty must face reality . . . put down his weaker feelings and act with strength and resolution . . . (Maximilian continues to read.) We must destroy the enemy before he can destroy us.

MAXIMILIAN (speaks with his back to Bazaine):

M'sieu le Maréchal—those who believe that they are fighting for their country are not to be used as criminals. The instinct which prompts patriotism is one of the noblest in human nature, and no man who possesses it is guilty in his soul.

BAZAINE:

But Your Majesty . . .

MAXIMILIAN:

The death penalty is not for those who act—however misguidedly—from principle . . . Would you proscribe men like the prisoner, General Díaz, for example . . . ? My physician, Dr. Basch, who attended his wound, says that the sincerity of Díaz is no more to be questioned than his military reputation. The empire will have a place for him—and others like him—when they can be convinced of my equal sincerity . . . It will not be on a gallows, M'sieu Maréchal. Sign this decree . . . never! (He tosses it aside.)

BAZAINE:

Your Majesty, I shall speak bluntly. We have no time to waste in putting down all resistance to your reign here. The American Civil War is over; and unless Your Majesty's government is established without opposition, the United States may decide that your presence in Mexico is a violation of the Monroe Doctrine.

MAXIMILIAN:

What has the Monroe Doctrine to do with my presence here? It applies only to the extension of European systems to the Americas . . . . I am not responsible to any power outside of Mexico.

BAZAINE:

The United States might hold otherwise.

MAXIMILIAN:

How can they? In the light of so democratic a means as the plebiscite upon which I accepted the throne?

BAZAINE:

Plebiscite! What significance has a plebiscite in a country like this, where eighty percent of the population can neither read nor write nor understand?

MAXIMILIAN (tonelessly):

Do you mean that the plebiscite was not a true expression of the desires of a vast majority of the Mexican people?

BAZAINE (brutally):

Most of the vast majority which voted in Your Majesty's favor were ignorant peons who didn't know who or what they were voting for.

MAXIMILIAN:

Am I to understand that coercion was used? (Bazaine indicates by expression and gesture that the answer is too obvious for words. Maximilian pulls a bell cord; a servant appears immediately at the door; to Bazaine.) We bid you good day, M'sieu le Maréchal.

BAZAINE:

But the decree . . .

MAXIMILIAN (harshly):

Good day . . . M'sieu le Maréchal.

The Frenchman turns on his heel to leave, but before he reaches the open doorway Carlotta enters. Bazaine clanks his spurs, bows stiffly, and exits. The empress looks after him and then turns an apprehensive and questioning regard toward her husband.

CARLOTTA:
What is it, Max'l?

MAXIMILIAN:
I have just learned something which places me as emperor of Mexico in a new and terrible light . . . The plebiscite was—as Juárez stated in his letter to me—a fraud . . . . The name of Hapsburg has been used to conceal an iniquitous enterprise. Napoleon has made us his dupes.

CARLOTTA:
He wouldn't dare, Max'l.

MAXIMILIAN:
Let us not deceive ourselves, Carlotta. We have been sufficiently deceived by others. I was brought to the throne of Mexico by a pretended plebiscite, and now I am expected to maintain myself upon it by the slaughter of subjects who neither acknowledged nor desired me.

CARLOTTA (in growing apprehension):
Max'l . . . my dear!

MAXIMILIAN:
I was brought to Mexico by Napoleon to destroy an adversary worthier than himself in every possible respect.

CARLOTTA:
Do you mean Benito Juárez?

MAXIMILIAN:
Yes, Carlotta . . . When I broke with my council over the land issue, one of the ministers accused me of speaking in the words of the Indian . . . As a consequence, I investigated the man— (indicating several legal tomes on his desk) his state papers, the Con-

stitution which he drafted, and the law which bears his name . . . They convinced me that the accusation of the minister was true: that I had spoken with the very words of Benito Juárez; and I am now convinced that I was brought to Mexico to destroy the very ideals which were my own fondest hopes for this nation.[46]

CARLOTTA:
If it is true, what is to be done?

MAXIMILIAN:
I have no choice—there is but one course in keeping with my honor . . .

CARLOTTA (slowly):
Do you mean . . . abdication? (He raises his eyes to hers.) Oh, Max'l . . .

MAXIMILIAN:
A Hapsburg is not a usurper.

CARLOTTA:
So final and vital a decision is not to be made in the heat of emotion . . . (So that he will not see her own distress, she turns away from him and, speaking, tries to make her tone impersonal but cannot altogether keep her voice from trembling.) Sovereignty is the most sacred obligation of man . . . (She is striving to order her thoughts and to express them logically.) By abdicating you may cause the world to think that you accepted the crown knowing full well the plebiscite was false, that after plotting with Napoleon you became fearful of failure and proclaimed your innocence at his expense . . . As an individual you could rise above such accusations, but they would not affect yourself alone—the dignity of the House of Hapsburg would suffer.

MAXIMILIAN:

Am I to impose myself upon a people for that reason?

CARLOTTA:

Is there a better? To bring blame upon the House of Hapsburg, and all it stands for, is to weaken the very institution of monarchy. You came forward as the savior of Mexico, to regenerate her people and uplift them . . . Will you abandon them to this bloody decree on the plea that they are not worthy of your efforts . . . that they have no need of your protection?

MAXIMILIAN:

God knows they need a sovereign—if for no other reason than to protect them against the greed and brutality of the Napoleons, the Bazaines, and the Montares . . .

CARLOTTA:

Max'l—what was the oath you swore when they placed the crown of Mexico on your head . . . ?

MAXIMILIAN:

To protect and defend her people—even to the shedding of my life's blood . . .

CARLOTTA:

Do so, then—show the world that no earthly consideration can keep you from fulfilling that oath . . . Think, Max'l, think—not of abandoning your country in her time of necessity—but of a way to deliver her from the hands of her enemies . . .

Maximilian makes no answer, and Carlotta watches him as he stands immobile, torn by his emotions. Hardly conscious of her, he commences to walk up and down the room. Suddenly he stops, and a light of decision appears on his face.

CARLOTTA:

Max'l—?

MAXIMILIAN:

There may be a way, Carlotta. I think there is a way . . .

She stands watching him as he strides determinedly from the room.

DISSOLVE TO:

104. FULL SHOT EXT. COURTYARD OF A PRISON NIGHT

A single big lantern partly illuminates the masonry. Over the scene the challenge of a sentry is heard, and after an inaudible answer, his voice calls:

SENTRY'S VOICE:

Commander of the guard!

From a shadow-hidden doorway an officer emerges into view, followed by a couple of soldiers. They cross the courtyard at a brisk gait, disappear from view, and the clang of heavy gates being opened sounds over the scene. The three then reappear, escorting a tall figure in a martial cloak.

CUT TO:

105. INT. OF A PRISON CELL

General Porfirio Díaz lies asleep on a cot. He is unshaven, and a wounded arm is bandaged to his chest. Over the scene sound steps coming along a corridor. Díaz's eyes open. The noise of the cell door being unlocked is heard, and Díaz turns his head in its direction.

CUT TO:

106–110. MED. SHOT SHOOTING OVER DÍAZ'S HEAD

Maximilian, in a long cloak, standing in the doorway. He nods a dismissal to his off-scene escort and waits until the sound of footsteps in the corridor dies away.

MAXIMILIAN:
General Porfirio Díaz . . . you know who I am . . . (When Díaz does not answer.) I am Maximilian von Hapsburg, emperor of Mexico.

DÍAZ (after some time):
Well . . . Maximilian—

MAXIMILIAN (sitting down):
I want to talk to you.

DÍAZ:
What have *we* got to talk about?

MAXIMILIAN:
Much, I think. (Again Díaz just waits, looking at him.) I deeply regret that this meeting had to take place in a prison cell.

DÍAZ:
Where else could it take place but in a prison cell or on the battlefield?

MAXIMILIAN (smiling):
Then from all accounts, señor, it is well for me that we meet here. If my generals are to be believed, you are the best soldier in Mexico.

DÍAZ:
I do not fight for glory . . . but for liberty.

MAXIMILIAN (nodding):
That is why I need your help.

DÍAZ:
My help . . . ? (In contemptuous suspicion.) At what price: Your Imperial favor . . . ? A command in your army . . . ? A medal, Maximilian . . . ? Or merely money . . . ?

MAXIMILIAN:
If any material consideration could buy you, General Díaz, I should not be here . . .

DÍAZ (grinning sardonically):
You want my help—my help . . .

MAXIMILIAN:
In bringing peace to Mexico.

DÍAZ:
Only one man can bring peace to Mexico—*Benito Juárez*.

MAXIMILIAN:
What is he—Benito Juárez—that he inspires such men as yourself, General Díaz? Tell me.

DÍAZ (after looking Maximilian over from head to foot):
What is he? He is an ugly little man in a black frock coat which doesn't fit . . . He is Benito Juárez. He was born in misery to live on a few grains of maize a day, to toil in the fields as a child, to grow up in ignorance and superstition, to be exploited by a white master . . . He is Benito Juárez . . . an Indian.

MAXIMILIAN (nodding):
He might be Mexico . . . I have read his works, but of the man himself I know nothing . . . Tell me more.

DÍAZ:
He labored for an education . . . He used it to help his own people and they elected him as their representative . . . He was imprisoned and exiled by a dictator, but he helped to destroy the dictator and free Mexico . . . He wrote the Constitution . . . He became president of Mexico . . . He ruled it justly and well, till traitors and landowners and speculators brought the French to depose him and put you in his place . . . You! Maximilian von Hapsburg!

MAXIMILIAN:

What is it that he seeks?

DÍAZ:

To put an end to the things he himself has endured. To liberate, to educate, to uplift, *through democracy.*

MAXIMILIAN:

Then all that lies between us is a word, General Díaz, for otherwise Benito Juárez and I are in accord.

DÍAZ:

A word . . . señor?

MAXIMILIAN:

Only a word—*democracy*. I agree with Benito Juárez that in theory it is the ideal system; but in practice government by the people can become the rule of a mob . . . a mob which follows whatever demagogue will promise most. From such as these, General Díaz, only a monarch can protect the state.

DÍAZ (somewhat interested):

Why a monarch more than a president?

MAXIMILIAN:

Because a president is a politician and must answer to his party. But a king is above factions and parties. A president may be poor and therefore open to temptation. But a king, having everything, desires nothing.

DÍAZ:

Do you mean there can be no such thing as a corrupt king? What about your Napoleon?

MAXIMILIAN:

Napoleon is not a true monarch, señor, any more than he is an aristocrat . . . Kings are born to their thrones—Napoleon took the crown of France by force . . . (Bitterly.) Napoleon is a dictator—and dictators do not govern with justice but with contempt. They despise men in order to be above men . . . they would make men lower and lower; for they gauge their own greatness by the scorn which they hold in their hearts for others. It is different with a king who is a king. A greater obligation rests upon him than upon those of lesser birth . . . the obligation to defend his own honor, which is the honor of his ancestors and the honor of his posterity as well.

DÍAZ:

You may be honest, Excelencia— (He approaches the emperor and looks into his eyes.) I believe you are . . . (With a casual gesture dismissing any impression which may have been made upon him.) But I am no político to understand such matters . . . And who can say what tyrant might follow you . . . sent by Napoleon. (As an afterthought.) You have no son, Excelencia.

111. CLOSE-UP MAXIMILIAN

He is profoundly shaken by the realization that this must be the attitude of every republican, and of what it will mean to Carlotta.

MAXIMILIAN (after a period of grim decision):

You have our promise as a Hapsburg that the succession will be regulated immediately, without foreign influence and in the best interest of the nation. (He walks to the barred window, looks out for a time, and then turns around.) General Díaz, will you carry a message for me to Benito Juárez?

DÍAZ:

A message—what message?

MAXIMILIAN:

Tell him I want him to be prime minister of Mexico.

As Díaz stands looking at him in astonishment

DISSOLVE TO:

112. EXT. LONG SHOT A SOLITARY HORSEMAN DAY
set against the magnificent Mexican landscape as he rides toward the north.

CUT TO:

113. EXT. MOVING CLOSE SHOT GENERAL PORFIRIO DÍAZ
as seen within the field of a pair of binoculars. He is mounted on a handsome palomino, equipped with saddle bags, and riding at the gait of one who is on a long journey.

CUT TO:

114. EXT. TERRACE AT CHAPULTEPEC
The wide stone balcony or terrace at Chapultepec, from which the great panorama of the mountains and the vale of Mexico is in view. Maximilian is in the act of setting down a pair of field glasses, through which he has been watching the departing Díaz. Carlotta is leaning on the broad balustrade by his side, wearing a white Spanish costume, with high comb and mantilla.[47] Exquisite in the brilliant sunshine.

MAXIMILIAN:

He should reach Juárez within three weeks' time.

CARLOTTA:

If he accepts, all Mexico will be in your hands— Napoleon, Bazaine, the Conservatives must bow to you . . . Oh, Max'l, what a sublime stroke of statecraft!

The distant sound of a song with mandolin accompaniment begins to be heard over the scene, faint, indistinguishable, and far away.

MAXIMILIAN:

It is destiny that I should join forces with the Indian . . . We are opposites—yes; but united opposites . . . like magnetic poles. We shall augment each other: nobility springs from the soil—and when it returns to the soil, it is revitalized . . . reborn.

CARLOTTA (worshipfully):

It is greatness, my dear—but not beyond the faith I had in your capacity to be great . . . You are going to be the enlightened ruler of a new era in monarchy.

The music and words of a song rise again—now clear, warm and vibrant—over the scene.

VOICE (over scene; singing):

Cuando salí de la Habana Válgame Diós . . .[48]

CARLOTTA (stretching her hand to the emperor, who takes it into his own):

Listen, Max'l . . .

The first verse of "La Paloma" is sung.

CUT TO:

115. TWO-SHOT ANOTHER ANGLE

with more of the background in evidence than in the previous shot.

MAXIMILIAN:

Beautiful . . .

CARLOTTA:

It is the most beautiful song I ever heard.

MAXIMILIAN:

Where does it come from . . . ? Who is singing?

CARLOTTA:

Who knows . . . The wife of a gardener . . . the sweetheart of some soldier . . .

MAXIMILIAN:

Mexico.

As the second verse of the song is sung Carlotta translates its words into English, looking at him with the wide, tender eyes of an enchanted child.

CARLOTTA:

If to your window there should come a dove . . . treat it tenderly . . . for it is I . . . Tell it of your love . . . my life's enchantment . . . Crown it with flowers . . . for it is I. (After a final chord from the guitar.) It must be terrible to be separated from one's love . . . I do not think I could live apart from you, Max'l . . .

MAXIMILIAN (tenderly):

We shall never be apart . . . (He takes her arm and they begin to stroll along the terrace.)

CARLOTTA:

To think all this began in Brussels, where a little girl with big, staring eyes used to follow you around her father's palace like a beagle . . . Oh, Max'l, it's like a fairy tale, isn't it? (Gestures toward the walls of Chapultepec.) Here stood the very halls of Montezuma—of the feathered emperor, himself! And there in the park below are living trees which actually saw him. What do they think about us, you and me, Max'l? (Maximilian makes no answer; his face has grown serious. But Carlotta does not notice the change of mood.) At this moment, I would be completely happy if . . .

MAXIMILIAN (stopping in reluctant decision, after watching her for a long time):

Carlotta—

CARLOTTA (turning to him):

Yes, Max'l?

MAXIMILIAN (taking her hands in his):

I am going to ask you to join me in a great sacrifice.

CARLOTTA (now aware of his constraint and growing alarmed):

A sacrifice . . . ?

MAXIMILIAN:

My advisers feel it is necessary that the nation should be given some assurance as to the succession, even if that insurance means that the crown will not pass to our own possible descendants.

CARLOTTA (the blood draining from her cheeks):

Max'l . . .

MAXIMILIAN:

You may recall having read of the ill-fated emperor [Agustín de] Iturbide, who attempted to establish a monarchy in Mexico some forty years ago . . . .[49] It appears there is a grandson of his—a mere child—whom my advisers think it might be well to consider . . . since he has some color of title to the crown.

CARLOTTA (her face a mask):

Is it so urgent, then?

MAXIMILIAN:

It would be a guarantee to the nation if we were to take this child of good Mexican blood under our protection and train him for the future.

CARLOTTA (her eyes begin to search his face in a new fear):

Under our protection? Do you mean—adopt?

MAXIMILIAN (in an affected, almost casual tone):

Oh, there would inevitably have to be some such legal formality.

CARLOTTA:

Max'l—with whom have you been consulting . . . ? Max'l . . . not with Basch? (She crumples in a fit of hopeless sobbing.) Not . . . with Basch?

MAXIMILIAN (himself equally broken at the dreadful hurt he has inflicted; putting an arm about her):

Carlotta . . . Charlotte . . . Perhaps in God's

infinite wisdom it is all for the best . . . Perhaps it is better that Mexico should have a successor of Mexican blood.

CARLOTTA (rising and freeing herself from him):
Send me away, Max'l . . . Marry someone who can give you a child—a Hapsburg son of your own . . . I love you enough to go—to be glad to go for your sake . . . I love you enough for anything.

Maximilian slowly takes her hands in his. Their eyes meet. Maximilian speaks with a quiet finality.

MAXIMILIAN:
There will be no child of my blood that is not yours, Charlotte.

In loving, humble gratitude, Carlotta impulsively goes into Maximilian's arms and clings to him.

CARLOTTA (after a time and almost in a whisper):
Let me arrange it, Max'l . . . Let me bring him to you—the little Iturbide—as though he were our own. (As her head comes away from his breast we see the tears in Carlotta's eyes.)

DISSOLVE TO:

116. EXT. LONG SHOT A SOLITARY HORSEMAN
Set against another magnificent landscape, General Porfirio Díaz rides on into the north.

DISSOLVE TO:

117. EXT. JUÁREZ'S HEADQUARTERS AT PASO DEL NORTE
It is an unpretentious house with a couple of guards, some squatting Indians, and a few other hangers-on about the entrance. General Díaz rides into the scene. He is dusty and travel worn, and his horse is almost worn out. There are exclamations of surprise as he dismounts and enters the building.

BYSTANDERS:
General Díaz. It is Porfirio Díaz, amigos. Heaven be praised, he has escaped.

CUT TO:

117A. INT. ANTEROOM OF JUÁREZ'S HEADQUARTERS

The room is filled with various Mexican types awaiting audiences with the president. A secretary is busy at his desk. There is another chorus of surprised exclamations as Díaz enters.

ALL:

General Díaz! You have escaped! Heaven be praised, amigos, it is Porfirio Díaz. Etc.

Díaz waves a greeting with his good arm, but makes no explanation of his presence. An excited secretary comes forward, leads the way to the door of an inner room, and throws it open. As the graven features of Juárez appear above his desk

CUT TO:

117B. INT. JUÁREZ'S OFFICE

with General Porfirio Díaz standing in the doorway. He has stopped on the threshold, the sight of the Indian having raised a qualm in his mind. As he moves toward the desk

DÍAZ:

It has been a long ride to reach you . . . here on the border.

JUÁREZ:

So you escaped, Porfirio?

DÍAZ (shaking his head):

No, Señor Juárez . . . (He pauses as though somewhat embarrassed.) I was *given* my freedom.

JUÁREZ (looking keenly at the soldier):

You were *given* your freedom?

DÍAZ:

Maximiliano ordered it . . . Maximiliano himself.

JUÁREZ (on his guard instantly):

You saw him?

DÍAZ (in a tone which is almost narrative and merely reflects his original emotion; at no time throughout the scene does he attempt to influence the Indian, except as to the truth of what is being told):

He came to the prison—to my cell—alone . . . He talked . . . At first I suspected trickery.

JUÁREZ (with eyes that are searching the soldier):

What did he talk about?

DÍAZ:

About his ideas of government . . . I doubted my own ears, for what I heard was you speaking—your words out of his mouth . . . Like you, Señor Juárez—he wants to help our people.

JUÁREZ:

How?

DÍAZ:

By protecting them from those who would oppress them.

JUÁREZ:

Virtue is a formidable weapon in the hands of an enemy.

DÍAZ:

He is not your enemy . . . Your aims are his aims . . . He says only a word—democracy!—lies between him and you.

JUÁREZ (grimly):

Only a word?

DÍAZ:

He is honest, Señor Juárez . . . You will know how honest when I tell you his message.

JUÁREZ:

So there is a message?

DÍAZ (after a pause):

He wants you to be prime minister of Mexico. In a monarchy founded upon the principles of your own Constitution.

JUÁREZ (not yet recovered):

It is the Constitution of a republic, Porfirio.

DÍAZ:

He swears he will defend its principles against the políticos and selfish interest . . . He says that such principles must always be defended by someone like himself . . . someone who is above all factions and parties . . .

JUÁREZ:

Maximiliano says only a word stands between him and me. Only the word democracy . . . What does it mean, Porfirio?

DÍAZ:

Democracy . . . ? Why, it means liberty, liberty for a man to say what he thinks. And to worship as one believes . . . and it is equal opportunity.

JUÁREZ:

No . . . that cannot be its meaning, Porfirio . . . Because Maximiliano offers us all these things *without* democracy . . . What is it then that he would withhold from us?

DÍAZ:

Only the right to rule ourselves . . .

JUÁREZ:

Then that must be the meaning of the word, Porfirio . . . the right to rule ourselves . . . The right of every man to rule himself and the nation in which he lives . . . And since no man rules himself into bondage . . . therefore liberty flows from it as water from the hills.

DÍAZ:

I understand, Señor Juárez.

JUÁREZ:

I say to entrust one's fate to a superior individual is to betray the very spirit of liberty. The spirit by which each man may raise himself to that level of human dignity where no man is the superior of any others . . . Where even the lowliest is uplifted to the worth of his manhood and is able to rule with wisdom, justice, and tolerance, toward *all* men. Should I now know it, Porfirio? Am I not of the lowliest?

DÍAZ:

You are right, Señor Juárez.

JUÁREZ:

Yes, only a word, *democracy*, may stand between Maximiliano von Hapsburg and myself . . . But it is an unbridgeable gulf . . . We represent irreconcilable principles . . . one or the other of which must perish . . . You see, Porfirio, when a monarch misrules, he changes the people; when a president misrules, the people change him . . .

DISSOLVE TO:

118. INT. STUDY

López and Bazaine are present. Maximilian enters, overjoyed.

MAXIMILIAN:

Maréchal Bazaine, we have received word from General Díaz that the answer of Benito Juárez will reach us at four o'clock this afternoon . . . (To López.) You will arrange for its delivery to us during the ceremonies, Colonel . . . (Turning to Bazaine.) Should it come before our appearance with the crown prince on the balcony, we shall make an important announcement to the crowd.

López exits.

BAZAINE:

Your Majesty committed a grievous error in releasing the prisoner Díaz.

MAXIMILIAN:

We do not believe we acted in error.

BAZAINE:

How can any reliance be placed on the word of Benito Juárez . . . You will be tricked—for the last time I implore Your Majesty to sign the decree authorizing me to take repressive measures.

MAXIMILIAN:

I told you that I will never sign such a decree.

Bazaine exits. Carlotta enters, leading little Iturbide by his hand.

AGUSTÍN (bows):

Your Majesty.

MAXIMILIAN:

Is Agustín von Hapsburg prepared for his investiture this afternoon?

AGUSTÍN:

Yes, Your Majesty.

MAXIMILIAN:

Has he memorized the words of his oath?

CARLOTTA (to Agustín):

Repeat them for your father . . .

Agustín starts to kneel down.

DISSOLVE TO:

119. THRONE ROOM CLOSE SHOT

of the kneeling Agustín, now robed and mantled, before Maximilian in his estate as emperor of Mexico, with Carlotta enthroned by his side.

AGUSTÍN:

I am thy liege man, of life and limb and earthly honor.

Then he kisses Maximilian's hand. As we pull back we see the archbishop Labastida. The audience all in court dress. Ladies-in-waiting, courtiers, among them Montares and all of the former cabinet members, Bazaine, officers, etc.

120. CLOSE SHOT MAXIMILIAN AND AGUSTÍN

Maximilian raises the child, kisses his cheek. Camera pulls back as Maximilian stands Agustín between himself and Carlotta. Then comes the acclamation: "Vive Agustín." A fanfare of trumpets and then the anthem. The emperor and the empress rise.

121. MOVING SHOT THE IMPERIAL GROUP

Maximilian and Carlotta lead the child toward the balcony. Camera holds at the doors leading out onto the balcony, and López comes close to Maximilian.

MAXIMILIAN:

Has no message arrived, López?

LÓPEZ:

Not yet, Your Majesty.

MAXIMILIAN:

Should it come, do not hesitate to bring it out to me . . . even at the last instant, López.

LÓPEZ:

Your Majesty—I beg of Your Majesty not to expose his person to the mob. There is no telling what some fanatic might attempt.

MAXIMILIAN (affectionately):

You Mexicans are unduly suspicious of one another.

Camera pans as they pass out onto the balcony, where they are greeted by a great shout.

CUT TO:

122. EXT. TERRACE FULL SHOT THE CROWD

Maximilian holds up his hand, and the throng becomes quiet.

CUT TO:

123. EXT. BALCONY CLOSE SHOT MAXIMILIAN

with the child in his arms. When the noise of the crowd subsides, Maximilian continues.

MAXIMILIAN:

Until this hour, we have been bound to Mexico by oaths of fealty and by the natural love a monarch feels for his people. Now another bond has been added, a bond of flesh and blood, since we, with our consort, have seen fit to assume the sacred obligations of parenthood. It is our happiness to present to you Agustín von Hapsburg, Crown Prince of Mexico. His person shall be a guarantee for the future of this realm—a future of peace, based firmly upon unity within Mexico, and not upon the presence of a foreign force.

His last words are hardly out before there is a terrific detonation, which causes the very palace to tremble.

CUT TO:

124. MED. SHOT BALCONY

The sound of the explosion is followed by rifle fire.

CUT TO:

125. LONG SHOT CROWD FROM BALCONY

The crowd turns in the direction of the sound. Those who are on the balcony stand as though rooted, watching a great column of smoke rising in the distance. Rifle fire commences to sound in the distance.

CUT TO:

126. MED. SHOT BALCONY
Agustín begins to cry. Maximilian, holding him in his arms, tries to comfort him.

LÓPEZ:
To your posts, officers of the guard!

Bugles are sounding the alarm. The rifle fire continues.

CUT TO:

127. MED. SHOT INT. THRONE ROOM
The imperial party turn back into the throne room. Maximilian, carrying the child, is confronted by Bazaine.

MAXIMILIAN:
What has happened, Maréchal?

An officer runs up.

OFFICER:
Juaristas disguised as citizens have overpowered the guard and blown up the powder magazines.

BAZAINE (Maximilian draws his watch, looks at it):
That is the answer you've been awaiting from Benito Juárez!

The firing in the distance becomes more rapid. Maximilian gives the child to Carlotta and starts toward his own suite. After a few paces he turns back to Bazaine.

MAXIMILIAN:
Maréchal Bazaine . . . (Bazaine goes to him.) The decree . . . (Holds out his hand. Maximilian takes the decree from Bazaine and, without answer, exits, followed by the maréchal.)

CUT TO:

128. CLOSE SHOT MAXIMILIAN
as he opens the decree on his desk, dips a quill into the ink. Bazaine stands over him. He signs.

FADE OUT

FADE IN

129. MONTAGE OF EXECUTIONS UNDER THE BLACK DECREE (ALREADY PHOTOGRAPHED)

Great winged vultures floating and wheeling in the sky. The camera pans down the facade of a church to its door, upon which is posted a legal notice, headed "Decree" and signed by Maximilian, Emperor of Mexico. A peon in the foreground reads a phrase or two of the illegible text to a companion.

PEON:

> It says that all republicans taken prisoner will be shot . . . It says that all people found with arms in their houses will be condemned and put to death within twenty-four hours . . . It says that . . .

DISSOLVE TO:

130. EXT. A WALL GROUP SHOT SIX BLINDFOLDED MEN (ALREADY PHOTOGRAPHED)

some with cigarettes between their lips, standing in line before a wall. Pull back to the rifles of a French firing party, leveled on the condemned men. An officer's voice is heard over the scene, giving the command:

OFFICER'S VOICE:

> Get ready . . . Aim . . . (and as a point directly behind the rifles is reached) Fire!

A cloud of powder smoke fills the screen.

DISSOLVE TO:

131. MED. SHOT EXT. A STREET IN A MEXICAN TOWN

A funeral procession is passing the camera. Coffin after coffin moves by—crude coffins carried by barefooted peons, each attended by a little group of mourning women and numerous brood. Through this we

DISSOLVE TO:

132. MED. SHOT A DIFFERENT STREET IN ANOTHER MEXICAN TOWN

The men of the town, old and young, are being herded forward in a column by French soldiers. Obviously they are to be new victims for the French firing squads. As they pass the camera some are telling their beads, their lips murmuring in prayer; others are stolid and resigned; still others, defiant and fearless.

The camera trucks toward the passing column to pick out Pepe marching with the others. As the camera moves with him we see his determined face as he looks furtively about him.

CUT TO:

133. MED. SHOT THE MOVING COLUMN OF PEONS
Pepe breaks from the column and races toward an alleyway between some of the houses that line the streets. A warning cry goes up from several of the soldiers.

CUT TO:

134. MED. CLOSE SHOT ONE OF THE SOLDIERS
calmly raises his rifle, takes aim, and fires.

CUT TO:

134A. MED. CLOSE SHOT PEPE
The impact of the bullet sprawls him flat against the wall of one of the buildings. On the wall, near one of Pepe's hands, a copy of the Black Decree is pasted. One of its corners flaps loosely, for the sun has dried up the paste. But we are able to see enough of the bold black letters of the heading of the Black Decree to recognize it.

Pepe slowly starts to crumple, and his hand in passing grips the poster and tears most of it from the wall as he slumps to the ground.

CUT TO:

134B. MED. LONG SHOT THE MARCHING COLUMN SHOOTING PAST PEPE
It continues on its way down the street.

CUT TO:

134C. MED. CLOSE SHOT PEPE ON THE GROUND
Recovering from the first shock, he gathers his strength and drags himself painfully along the wall and into the alleyway.

WIPE TO:

134D. INT. JUÁREZ'S HOUSE IN PASO DEL NORTE

Juárez sits behind his desk, stonelike, listening grimly to a secretary who is reading to him from a bundle of dispatches in his hand.

SECRETARY:

"In Uruapan they filled the corral with townsmen and stood off and fired volley after volley into their midst . . ." (Reading from another dispatch.) "In San Luis Potosí the dead hanging from the trees lined the road for two leagues into the city . . ."

CUT TO:

134E. MED. CLOSE SHOT EXT. FRONT DOOR OF JUÁREZ'S HOUSE IN PASO DEL NORTE

A grizzled, ragged peon, his face tense, is knocking anxiously on the door. It is opened by Camilo. The peon blurts out to him:

PEON:

Camilo—come quickly! It's your boy Pepe—we found him wounded—on the road from Chihuahua!

As the peon indicates with a gesture behind him and Camilo follows it with a glance

CUT TO:

134F. MED. SHOT THE STREET SHOOTING PAST CAMILO AND THE PEON

A dilapidated cart, drawn by mules, stands at the curb. The wounded Pepe, weak from the loss of blood, his clothes torn and dirty, is being supported by another peon as they cross toward Camilo. Seeing them, Camilo cries in alarm as he runs toward Pepe.

CAMILO:

Pepe! (He takes the boy in his arms.)

PEPE (shaking his head; with a desperate determination he gasps):

Take me to Don Benito—I must tell him—

CUT TO:

134G. MED. SHOT INT. JUÁREZ'S HOUSE

He looks up quickly as through one of the doors of the room Camilo comes in with Pepe and the two peons. With a grim effort, Pepe frees himself from his father's arms, squares himself, and crosses unsteadily to Juárez at the desk in the foreground.

PEPE (every word an effort):

Don Benito—the French took Chihuahua—burned the villages—shot the men— They said it was the law—

CUT TO:

134H. CLOSER SHOT PEPE SHOOTING PAST JUÁREZ

Taking the crumpled copy of the Black Decree from his shirt, he holds it toward Juárez.

PEPE (continuing; his strength leaving him):

—because it is written here—all men with arms—

He sinks to the floor, his head disappearing behind the desk, with the hand in which he clutches the Black Decree resting on the edge of the desk.

Juárez leans over, loosens the fingers of the boy's hand, and takes the Black Decree from it. As he straightens up and stands holding it his face is a stone mask.

CUT TO:

134I. WIDER ANGLE THE ROOM

Camilo, his grief too keen for tears, crosses to the desk and picks up the body of Pepe in his arms and goes out of the room, followed by the two peons and the secretary.

CUT TO:

134J–K. CLOSER SHOT JUÁREZ AT DESK

His jaws set hard, he carefully opens the crumpled copy of the decree, smooths it flat on the desk. Then he folds it in four parts and puts it in the inside pocket of his coat. As he slowly sits down in his chair

CUT TO:

134L. WIDER ANGLE

Tejada enters by a door other than the one used by Camilo. He crosses to Juárez.

TEJADA:

Don Benito, there are some Americanos here to see you . . . They have come all the way from Washington— (He tenders a card.)

JUÁREZ (after looking at it):

From Washington? (Then squaring himself.) Let the señores come in.

Tejada crosses back to the door, opens it.

TEJADA (calling through the doorway):

If you please, señores.

Senator Harris enters with his friends, Roberts and Hartman.

HARRIS (crossing to Juárez and pumping his hand):

Mr. President!

JUÁREZ:

Mr. Harris, I presume.

HARRIS (deferentially):

Let me present Mr.Hartman and Mr. Roberts.

JUÁREZ:

Gentlemen, I am honored . . . Will you be seated?

Roberts and Hartman cross to chairs and sit down.

CUT TO:

134M. CLOSER SHOT THE GROUP

HARRIS (holding the back of a chair before sitting down):

Let me first express our admiration for you personally, Mr. President, no less than for the cause which you are defending. The blood of every decent man boils at this infamous Black Decree and the straits to which it has brought the republic.

Juárez stiffens a little.

HARTMAN:

It has roused the indignation of the entire United States, Your Excellency.

JUÁREZ:

Are you gentlemen, perhaps, from our benefactors, the Society of the Friends of Mexican Democracy?

HARRIS (after a look at his associates):

The Society of the Friends of Mexican Democracy . . . ?

ROBERTS:

Never heard of them.

JUÁREZ (puzzled):

But surely, gentlemen . . .? Their contributions have alone made it possible for us to go on.

HARRIS:

Contributions . . . ? Strange we have heard nothing of this in Washington.

JUÁREZ (with his own meaning):

Strange, indeed.

HARTMAN:

May I inquire as to size and number of these contributions?

JUÁREZ:

We have received to date about half a million pesos.

ROBERTS:

Only half a million pesos . . . Little enough in terms of your needs, I should think.

HARRIS:

You deserve better than that from the United States.

HARTMAN:

And we are here to offer it, Your Excellency!

CUT TO:

134N. ANOTHER ANGLE JUÁREZ AND GROUP

ROBERTS (getting down to business):
Mr. President . . . What are your requirements?

JUÁREZ (as he looks around the bare room):
We need five dollars . . . and we need five million dollars.

ROBERTS:
You shall have ten million dollars.

Juárez gives him a quick glance.

HARRIS:
Twenty million pesos.

HARTMAN:
We are prepared to establish a credit in that amount with any New York bank you care to name.

HARRIS:
Because of the idealistic nature of the transaction, we have arranged to underwrite the loan at the lowest possible rate—say, two and a half percent—redeemable in sixty-six years.

Juárez, realizing that he is being high pressured, probes them cagily.

JUÁREZ:
The Republic of Mexico will be under eternal obligation to you.

HARTMAN (with a pointed smile):
Not "eternal" we hope, Mr. President—only for sixty-six years.

ROBERTS:
Naturally, such a loan will have to be secured . . . But we have in mind a *way* of securing it which will prove of inestimable benefit to Mexico herself.

JUÁREZ (with apparent interest):
Indeed, gentlemen?

HARRIS (expansively):

What is Mexico's most crying need today! (He pauses dramatically.) Unquestionably the development of her natural resources, Mr. President! And why are they undeveloped? Mexico's natural resources are undeveloped for lack of capital!

JUÁREZ (nailing him down):

What security do you have in mind?

ROBERTS (his eyes on Juárez):

A monopoly over all the natural resources of the state of Sonora.

JUÁREZ:

Tell me, gentlemen—are you here as representatives of your government or in a private capacity?

ROBERTS:

We represent a syndicate of New York financiers, Mr. President.

JUÁREZ:

I'm sorry, gentlemen. I am quite unable to meet the terms you ask . . . irrespective of the benefits involved.

The three exchange anxious glances.

ROBERTS (trying to bargain):

Then what terms will you consider, Mr. President? Perhaps for the mineral rights alone—

JUÁREZ:

No, gentlemen . . . (Rising from his chair.) It is unfortunate that you must return to the United States without anything but my thanks. It is beyond my power as president of Mexico to barter the heritage of her future generations. (He offers his hand to Harris in a gesture of dismissal.)

CUT TO:

134O. WIDER ANGLE

JUÁREZ (to the group):

Is there anything I can do to add to your personal comfort while you are among us?

HARRIS (losing his amiability):

I think not, Mr. President . . . There is nothing else to detain us on this side of the border.

JUÁREZ:

Then, adiós, señores.

With curt bows Harris and his friends hurry out the door. Juárez crosses slowly from his desk to the window. As he stands staring out Tejada comes into the room.

TEJADA (a little anxiously):

Well, Don Benito . . . are we getting help from the Americanos?

CUT TO:

134P. CLOSER SHOT JUÁREZ AND TEJADA

JUÁREZ (without turning):

They were not Americanos, Tejada.

TEJADA (puzzled):

Not Americanos?

JUÁREZ:

Not Americanos but speculators . . . Speculators have no country. Those men were of the same breed that brought the French and Maximilian to Mexico.[50]

DISSOLVE TO:

135. CLOSE SHOT NAPOLEON III DAY

in a martial attitude on the saddle of a life-sized, white, wooden horse. Pull back to show him in a well-lighted room in the Tuileries, with an artist at work on a large canvas of the emperor and his marshals (viz, frontispiece to *The Gaudy Empire* by Alfred Neuman). The painting, which is all but completed, shows not the dropsical figure on the wooden horse but the young emperor of Solferino and Magenta days. A secretary comes in.

SECRETARY:

His Excellency, Mr. John Bigelow, minister from the United States of North America, Your Imperial Majesty.

Mr. Bigelow enters. He is a Yankee type in a frock coat who inspects the emperor on his perch without curiosity, clears his throat, and makes a short bow.

NAPOLEON:

Your Excellency will forgive the informality of this reception, but Monsieur Meissonier's canvas must be completed for the opening of the salon, he insists . . . (Napoleon gestures toward the artist, who bobs a bow over his palette and resumes work as though irritated by the interruption.) It seemed more important to comply with Your Excellency's urgent request for an audience than to stand on ceremony . . .

BIGELOW:

Indubitably, Your Majesty . . . (Little Mr. Bigelow begins to take on somewhat of a gamecock attitude.) I have been instructed from Washington by the secretary of state . . .

NAPOLEON (gesturing with his long-tubed cigarette):

Ah . . . that excellent M'sieu Seward . . .

BIGELOW:

. . . to ask you why the French flag is still in Mexico.

NAPOLEON (spreading his hands apart):

But M'sieu Seward is already aware of the circumstances. The former government of Mexico repudiated its legal debts to French investors . . . We sent an armed force into the country to seize the customs and collect what is due.

BIGELOW:

Do these collections involve the wholesale execution of Mexican loyalists under what is known as the Black Decree? (Napoleon coughs and squirms in the saddle.)

MEISSONIER (who is paying no attention to the conversation):

If Your Majesty pleases . . . (Napoleon adjusts his position.)

NAPOLEON:

The responsibility for the Black Decree is the emperor Maximilian's . . . It was conceived by him and executed by his own Mexican detachments.

BIGELOW:

What is your connection with this archduke Maximilian who calls himself Emperor of Mexico?

NAPOLEON (after a considerable pause):

The . . . er . . . archduke is an Austrian, of course, and claims independent sovereignty . . . French troops have aided him to maintain order only so that the collection of debts may be made.

BIGELOW:

Your Majesty is aware that under the Monroe Doctrine . . .

NAPOLEON:

I do not see how the Monroe Doctrine has any bearing upon the present circumstances in Mexico . . .

BIGELOW:

My government takes a contrary view . . . and is now prepared to enforce it—if necessary. General [Ulysses S.] Grant has been ordered to concentrate four army corps on the Mexican border . . .[51] How soon will Your Majesty's "collections" in Mexico be completed?

NAPOLEON (after chewing the tube of his cigarette to pulp):

Shortly . . . very shortly, I think. The matter would appear, to all intents and purposes, to be approaching a conclusion.

BIGELOW:

It is to be hoped so, Your Majesty, since my government has sanctioned the raising of a thirty-million-dollar loan for the equipment of the republican armies in Mexico. (Napoleon coughs, this time in real earnest. Mr. Bigelow bows abruptly and makes his exit.)

MEISSONIER (still engrossed in his work and oblivious to what has taken place):

If Your Majesty will be good enough to resume his martial pose . . .

DISSOLVE TO:

136. GROUP SHOT INT. OFFICE OF JUÁREZ AT PASO DEL NORTE

The Indian is seated at his desk, upon which are files of papers, maps, and other evidences of intense labor. With him are Escobedo, Díaz, Uradi, and Negroni.

JUÁREZ:

We may consider the equipment for the army of the north as complete, then, General Escobedo?

ESCOBEDO:

It will be complete as soon as General Carbajal takes over ten more batteries of American field guns at Matamoros.[52]

JUÁREZ:

And the armies of the west and the center?

ESCOBEDO (holding up a dispatch in his hand):
Word from Tejada in New Orleans assures me that a shipment of rifles will reach Matamoros within the week. Corona and Palacio will be ready to move as soon as we can get the rifles to them.

JUÁREZ (turning to Díaz):
And now—General Díaz, what are your needs for the army of the south?

DÍAZ:
Army of the south? Señor Presidente, there is no army of the south.

JUÁREZ:
You are the army of the south.

CUT TO:

137. ANOTHER ANGLE THE GROUP
Secretary enters with a sheet of paper in his hand. He crosses to the desk and places the paper before Juárez.

SECRETARY:
Señor Presidente, your message to the people regarding the help from the United States is ready for your signature.

Juárez picks up the paper and glances through it.

URADI (turning to Juárez):
Don Benito—you cannot sign it.

JUÁREZ (looking up at him):
And why not?

URADI (as if reluctant to tell him):
Because—your term of office has expired—you no longer have the legal power to act—you no longer are president.

There is a tense silence for a moment as all eyes go to Uradi.

138. CLOSER SHOT THE GROUP

NEGRONI (to Uradi):

You have in mind the constitutional provision that in the absence of an election, the vice-president shall succeed to the presidency?

URADI (with a little shrug):

I defer to Don Benito in all things relating to the Constitution—since he wrote it. The date for a presidential election is, however, some five months past.

ESCOBEDO (a little angrily):

How could an election have been held with the country in the hands of the enemy?

DÍAZ (before Uradi can answer):

And why did you make no mention of this matter before now, Señor Vice-Presidente? (Pointedly.) Is it because you preferred to sit back and wait until the plum was ripe for picking?

URADI (to Juárez; disregarding Díaz's thrust):

It is not a question of my aspiring to the office—but whoever holds it must have the power to act with absolute legality, if the country's affairs are to be carried on.

DÍAZ:

What you forget, señor, is that when Congress was forced to disband, it bestowed plenary powers upon Señor Juárez to defend the Constitution of Mexico. He cannot relieve himself of that duty until it is possible for Congress to meet again.

URADI:

Do you consider that such plenary powers were intended to extend beyond your legal term of office?

JUÁREZ (with quiet determination):
I do.

URADI:
Others will challenge that opinion.

CUT TO:

139. WIDER ANGLE
Díaz, losing his temper, grabs Uradi and pulls him up to him.

DÍAZ:
If you dare to jeopardize the cause for your personal ambition, I'll let the breath out of your throat.

JUÁREZ (separating them):
No, Porfirio—you must not misunderstand Alejandro. The question he raises cannot be answered with bitterness— (Turning and riveting his eyes on Uradi, Juárez continues in a friendly but ominous tone.) You must respect his sincerity—for he is a compañero—and old friend of the cause. He has fought long and well for its success— He would do nothing to betray it now— Is that not so, Alejandro?

URADI (uncomfortably):
Of course, Don Benito.

Juárez proffers Uradi his hand, and as he takes it Juárez pulls him to him and locks him in a grim abrazo.

DISSOLVE TO:

140. CLOSE SHOT A SIGN
on the exterior of a building that reads: Presidio de Matamoros. The camera pans down and pulls back to disclose a:

140A. MED. LONG SHOT EXT. THE PLAZA BEFORE THE HEADQUARTERS BUILDING
It is a scene of busy and noisy activity. Cases of rifles and munitions are being unloaded from wagons and

stacked in orderly piles. More wagons are arriving, heavily loaded with additional military supplies. On one side of the square are parked shiny new pieces of artillery with their caissons and limbers. More are being wheeled into place as they arrive.

CUT TO:

140B. MED. SHOT EXT. FRONT ENTRANCE TO HEADQUARTERS BUILDING

An open carriage pulls up and from it alights a man, obviously an American. He is greeted effusively by General Negroni, who is standing nearby with several of his staff, checking the inventory of the arriving supplies.

NEGRONI (as he crosses and shakes hands with the man):

Ah, Señor Lane. The presidente has been impatiently awaiting your arrival.

LANE:

Sorry, but I was detained getting further instructions from my government in Washington on several matters that I must bring to the attention of your president.

NEGRONI (after a moment's hesitation):

Of course, señor. (Indicating for him to follow.) At once.

As they go into the building

CUT TO:

140C. INT. AN OFFICE IN THE HEADQUARTERS AT MATAMOROS
MED. CLOSE SHOT THE DOORS LEADING INTO THE OFFICE

As Negroni comes through doors with Lane, Negroni announces off-scene:

NEGRONI:

Señor Presidente—the envoy from the United States.

LANE:

Your Excellency, I—

As he stops in surprise the camera pans from him to the desk where we see Uradi standing.

URADI (with a formal smile):

Please be seated, Señor Lane.

CUT TO:

140D. WIDER ANGLE

LANE (puzzled and confused):

I beg your pardon, Señor Uradi, but I was told I would find President Juárez here.

URADI (stiffly):

By virtue of the provisions of the Constitution, señor, I am now President of the Republic of Mexico.

As Lane stares at him dumbfoundedly[53]

DISSOLVE TO:

141. EXT. A FARMHOUSE NUEVO LEÓN DAY

It is serving as Escobedo's headquarters. In the background Juárez's carriage can be seen. The Indian, Escobedo, Carbajal, and two or three staff officers are at a table under a tree. Lerdo de Tejada rides into the scene on horseback. He is accompanied by a servant, who leads off his horse.

CARBAJAL:

You return at an evil hour, Señor Tejada . . . The munitions which you purchased for us in the United States have been seized by Uradi and—

TEJADA (nodding):

I have heard, compañero. (Then to Juárez.) Don Benito, you told me to investigate the Friends of Mexican Democracy when I reached New Orleans. There is no society of that name! Growing suspicious, I asked the American government for assistance. It ordered the bank to reveal the source of the monies we have been receiving . . . (Tejada pauses as he hands Juárez some papers he has taken from the briefcase he has brought with him.) These reports prove beyond question that all remittances came from Señor José Montares in Mexico City . . .

His listeners—save Juárez—turn and look at one another in disbelief. "From Montares . . . ?" "From the landowners . . . !" Escobedo and Carbajal exclaim.

TEJADA (continuing and dropping his bombshell):
And the last of them was made payable to Presidente Alejandro Uradi at Matamoros . . .

JUÁREZ (grimly):
So Uradi is a traitor . . .

CARBAJAL (banging his fist on the table):
We must plan a surprise attack on Matamoros. Let us get his ears if it's the last thing we ever do!

JUÁREZ (shaking his head):
No. If we move on Matamoros, Bazaine is certain to strike at our rear . . . Without munitions we shall be defenseless after a few days' fighting . . . Our forces will be dispersed . . . and it will be the end of the republican cause.

ESCOBEDO:
We could go back to guerrilla warfare.

JUÁREZ:
No, Mariano. With two claiming the presidency, we should be divided within and discredited without.

ESCOBEDO:
But we are not going down without a fight, Don Benito . . . whoever we fight.

JUÁREZ (rising):
There is only one hope, señores.

ESCOBEDO:

What hope, Don Benito?

JUÁREZ (as he folds the reports):

That I can get to Matamoros alone . . . before Bazaine strikes.

ALL (in chorus):

To Matamoros? To Uradi? To what purpose?

JUÁREZ:

We shall see . . .

CARBAJAL:

It is like an ant walking into the nest of a tarantula . . . He will kill you, Don Benito.

JUÁREZ (signaling to Juan on the box of the carriage):

That may be.

As the carriage begins to roll toward the group

DISSOLVE TO:

142–46. OMITTED

147. CLOSE SHOT CHAMBER OF THE EMPEROR'S SUITE CHAPULTEPEC

Maximilian, pale and exhausted, is being examined by Basch, who is listening to the emperor's heart action. Finally the little doctor straightens up, unscrews his trumpetlike stethoscope, and puts it in a case, while Maximilian rebelts his dressing gown.

BASCH:

There is nothing organically wrong with Your Majesty. Heart, lungs, liver are functioning perfectly. Still, Your Majesty is a very sick man. The older I grow in my profession, the more certain I become that there are sicknesses—some deadly—which are not physical by origin.

MAXIMILIAN:

You mean that anxiety has worn me down?

BASCH:

The continual state of tension which has been Your Majesty's existence since you signed the decree has undoubtedly had its effect; but I do not believe that mental stress is the true cause of your condition.

MAXIMILIAN:

What, then?

BASCH:

Your whole life here. Your Majesty is out of harmony with his environment; and by environment I do not mean simply altitude, temperature, humidity—but rather a thing of the spirit.

MAXIMILIAN:

Really, Basch—transcendentalism—and I believed you a man of exact science!

BASCH:

Your Majesty will remember the cats in Venice—the thousands upon thousands of cats . . . It is a veritable cat heaven. The narrow ways, courts, the very eaves are alive with them. They are born to thrive, breed, and never die. But a dog brought to Venice from the mainland grows melancholy, sickens, and inevitably dies—killed by his natural antipathy for cats. The feline nature is beyond the comprehension of a dog—its bloodthirst, its savage grace, its very perfection. One cat a dog will destroy; but when there are thousands, the thousands overcome his spirit.

MAXIMILIAN (rising):

My dear Samuel, I require a prescription, not a parable.

Camera pans with him as he moves nervously about the room. Basch, following him, enters the picture.

BASCH:

Very well. I prescribe that Your Majesty shall leave Mexico by the first boat—otherwise Mexico will kill you, one way or another.[54]

Carlotta enters, followed by López.

CARLOTTA (excited):

Max'l—good news!

LÓPEZ:

Uradi has broken away from Juárez! The enemy armies are in rebellion!

MAXIMILIAN (turning to López):

Has this been verified, Colonel?

LÓPEZ:

Beyond all question, Your Majesty . . . Uradi has captured the *Juarista* munitions base at Matamoros, and all the supplies from the United States are pouring into his hands.

MAXIMILIAN:

Uradi dares to oppose Juárez!

LÓPEZ:

It is the old story, Your Majesty—a political squabble involving the presidency—as if there *were* any such thing!

MAXIMILIAN (to López):

This is our opportunity . . . Bazaine will strike now and bring hostilities to an end.

López exits.

CARLOTTA:

Victory, Max'l—it means victory!

MAXIMILIAN:

Yes, victory—victory . . . Did you hear, Basch?

BASCH:

Yes, Your Majesty, I heard.

He withdraws. Maximilian and Carlotta are left alone. Maximilian puts his hand to his head in a gesture of exhaustion. Carlotta moves quickly to him.

CARLOTTA:

It is your own faith which is to be thanked for what has happened, Max'l.

Camera pans as Maximilian sinks into a chair, covers his face with his hands in trembling exhaustion.

148. CLOSE SHOT MAXIMILIAN AND CARLOTTA

Carlotta holds his head to her body.

CARLOTTA:

Poor Max'l. (Comfortingly.) Now we can come back to the world of reality as man and wife.

Carlotta kisses him. Agustín enters from the terrace with a butterfly net and large butterfly in it.

AGUSTÍN:

Look, Your Majesty! A butterfly!

Maximilian takes the net to examine the contents.

CARLOTTA:

See—he always comes to you. It makes me quite jealous.

MAXIMILIAN (smiling):

Nothing is so flattering as a child's spontaneous affection.

CARLOTTA (looking at Agustín tenderly):

It really is as though he were our own.

AGUSTÍN:

Isn't it beautiful, Your Majesty?

Maximilian strokes the child's head.

MAXIMILIAN (with some self-conscious pride):

Agustín, when we are alone together I wish you to call us Mother and Father.

AGUSTÍN:
When we are alone?

MAXIMILIAN:
Yes . . . It is only out of respect for others . . . when others are present . . . that you must address us as they do.

AGUSTÍN:
Yes, Your Majesty—I mean, Father.

López appears.

LÓPEZ:
M'sieu le Maréchal Bazaine.

MAXIMILIAN:
We shall receive him. (Turning to Agustín; for Agustín's benefit.) The crown prince of Mexico has our leave to withdraw. (Seeing Agustín's disappointment.) Tomorrow we shall catch butterflies together.

Bazaine enters. Agustín, upon seeing him, draws the emperor's head down.

AGUSTÍN:
Tomorrow . . . (Whispering.) Father . . .

After this, he runs out. Maximilian, now turning to Bazaine and addressing him more friendly than ever before.

MAXIMILIAN:
I have already heard the news, Maréchal. The enemy is at your mercy. No doubt you are leaving for the North to deliver the final blow in person.

Instead of an answer, Bazaine hands Maximilian a dispatch.

BAZAINE:
With Your Majesty's permission.

149. INSERT THE DISPATCH IN MAXIMILIAN'S HAND
to show that its envelope bears the signet of Napoleon III.

CUT TO:

150. CLOSE-UP MAXIMILIAN
as he opens and reads the letter. His hands begin to tremble a little.

151. GROUP SHOT MAXIMILIAN, CARLOTTA, AND BAZAINE

CARLOTTA:
Max'l . . . what is it?

Maximilian finishes reading and passes her the letter.

MAXIMILIAN (after a silence):
Do you know what this letter contains, Maréchal?

BAZAINE:
I have some idea, Your Majesty . . . (He pauses.) My orders are to concentrate all French troops for an immediate evacuation of Mexico.[55]

CARLOTTA (returning the letter):
Infamous!

MAXIMILIAN:
Do you mean that you will withdraw your forces at a moment when complete victory is within your grasp?

BAZAINE:
I am a soldier, Your Majesty, and must obey orders.

MAXIMILIAN:
There is a treaty between Napoleon and myself—the Treaty of Miramar—which guarantees that French troops shall remain in Mexico until the empire has been made secure. Your emperor has no power to withdraw from it without our consent. We deny his authority to do so, and— (tearing the letter in two) we refuse to receive his communication.

BAZAINE:

That is between Your Majesty and my Imperial Master. It cannot affect my actions.

MAXIMILIAN:

M'sieu le Maréchal, what you are about to do will leave a spot upon the honor of France which time can never wash away.

CUT TO:

152. THREE-SHOT

centered on Carlotta as she stands watching her husband.

CARLOTTA (turning toward Bazaine):

So you would leave us to the mercy of our enemies?

BAZAINE:

There is no question of being left to the mercy of enemies . . . His Majesty can abdicate and leave Mexico under the protection of the French army.

MAXIMILIAN (drawing himself up and freezing at the suggestion):

Since signing the decree, M'sieu le Maréchal, I have a responsibility to Mexico that may not be shirked . . . a responsibility for the slaughter in which you indulged under the authority of my name . . . No, I shall not abdicate.

CARLOTTA (breaking in):

Nor will you evacuate Mexico, M'sieu le Maréchal. (In a growing crescendo of fury.) Because I am going to Paris to confront your Napoleon with his obligation under the Treaty of Miramar . . . Because, if he refuses to live up to them, I am going to expose him before the courts of Europe . . . Because I will let the world know how we were lured to Mexico by misrepresentation and false promises—how he used the name of Hapsburg to give face to a shady enterprise . . . And because it will be the ruin of your master— M'sieu le Maréchal—if you dare to move a man.

MAXIMILIAN (to Bazaine):

M'sieu le Maréchal has our leave to withdraw.

The Frenchman clicks his spurs and exits.

153. CLOSE TWO-SHOT CARLOTTA AND MAXIMILIAN

CARLOTTA:

It was I who said to you at Miramar, "Accept the crown . . ." Because I believed in your capacity to rule—It was I who said, "Do not abdicate . . ." because I believed you alone could save Mexico from her oppressors— You are not at fault in anything . . . I alone am responsible. (Very simply.) And I will help you now.

DISSOLVE TO:

154. LONG SHOT THE IMPERIAL COACH, OTHER CARRIAGES, AND ESCORT IN FRONT OF TERRACE

The imperial coach and a cortege of less ornate vehicles are seen with an escort of Emperatriz Dragoons.

155. INT. IMPERIAL COACH

Maximilian and Carlotta approach the coach, with them Agustín. Maximilian lifts Carlotta's hand to his lips. Then they embrace.

CARLOTTA:

It will not be for long, Max'l.

MAXIMILIAN:

I cannot imagine existence without you.

CARLOTTA:

Our thoughts will bridge the distance between us. My own will never leave you, Max'l. Open your soul to me and I shall be with you, kneeling beside you in the chapel, riding beside you in the park of a morning, walking beside you at dusk by the Pool of the Concubines.

MAXIMILIAN:

My soul shall always be open to your love, Charlotte. (There is a long kiss.)

There is a pause, neither quite knowing what to say.

CARLOTTA:

Promise me you will obey Basch, Max'l, and be careful of your health in every way.

MAXIMILIAN:

I promise.

CARLOTTA:

Take your quinine regularly . . .

Maximilian, who is quite unable to speak, merely nods in answer.

CARLOTTA (in kissing Agustín):

And little Agustín—don't spoil him too much . . .

There is a pause.

156. MED. CLOSE SHOT EXT. CARRIAGE

Maximilian gives a signal for the escort to start. The command "Forward!" sounds, and the framed face of the empress is swept off-scene.

CAMERA PULLS BACK TO:

157. MED. SHOT MAXIMILIAN'S FULL FIGURE AND AGUSTÍN

as they stand watching the departing coach.

DISSOLVE TO:

158. LONG SHOT JUÁREZ'S FAMILIAR COACH

approaching the camera at a steady trot along a rocky road. It disappears around a bend in a plume of dust.

159. JUÁREZ'S COACH

rounding the bend. The camera pans with the familiar

dusty carriage past cacti forms in the foreground. Camilo, its driver, is tired and dirty. As the coach passes the camera a signpost is seen, bearing the words Matamoros, 3 Leagues.

DISSOLVE TO:

160. EXT. A CUSTOMS HOUSE BY THE ROADSIDE ON THE OUTSKIRTS OF MATAMOROS
with a picket of soldiers squatting, sleeping, and lounging before its door. At the appearance of the coach in the near distance, three of them pick up rifles and shamble out to the road.

161. THE APPROACHING CARRIAGE
shooting from behind a soldier, who is in the center of the roadway, while two others wait on either side of it. The carriage slows down to a stop and the two go up to its windows, ask some unintelligible question, and evidently receive an answer which astounds them; as after an instant of hesitation, one of them shouts, "It is Benito Juárez!" Voices off-scene take up the name, and the remainder of the picket rush past the camera toward the carriage.

162. CLOSER SHOT SIDE ANGLE THE CARRIAGE
A sergeant at its window, looking inside with an incredulous expression on his face.

JUÁREZ'S VOICE (from within):
I want to see Señor Uradi.

The picket closes in behind the sergeant.

VOICES OF THE SOLDIERS:
It *is* he . . . It is Juárez . . . It is Don Benito.

CUT TO:

163. INT. URADI'S HEADQUARTERS IN MATAMOROS
Uradi is gesticulating before a mirror, practicing a written speech which lies convenient to hand for consulta-

tion. Le Marc sits near him, watching with cynical amusement.

URADI:

. . . this resurrection of the true spirit of constitutional government . . . (He pauses, hand upraised in the air, having forgotten what follows, consults the script in that attitude, and resumes.) This termination of a dictatorship in the guise of democracy . . .

He tries it over several times with alternating gestures. There is an impatient rap at the door, which opens on General Negroni with several members of his staff and the breathless picket sergeant.

NEGRONI (tensely):

Señor Presidente . . . Benito Juárez . . . is entering Matamoros!

URADI (his jaw drops):

You mean we are being attacked?

SERGEANT:

No, no, Señor Presidente . . . he is alone in his carriage.

URADI:

Are you out of your senses?

SERGEANT:

It is Juárez, Señor Presidente . . . I spoke to him . . .

URADI (staggered):

What did he say?

SERGEANT:

Only that he wanted to see you.

URADI:

And he is alone . . . alone?

SERGEANT:

Except for his coachman.

URADI:

You fool! You should have arrested him!

CUT TO:

164. PAN SHOT JUÁREZ'S CARRIAGE
moving slowly through the outskirts of the city, with an escort of two soldiers and a small crowd following. As the carriage passes other people are seen running up.

VOICES OF CROWD:

It is Benito Juárez!

CUT TO:

165. INT. URADI'S HEADQUARTERS
MED. SHOT URADI, NEGRONI, AND LE MARC

NEGRONI:

Why should he put his life in our hands . . . ? He must know we will never let him get away alive.

URADI (with mounting anxiety):

It is some kind of a trick.

LE MARC (trying to reassure him):

Perhaps he has come to make a bargain with you . . .

URADI (nervously):

The Indian does not bargain . . .

NEGRONI:

Listen!

In the silence at his word, shouting is heard from the street outside. Uradi jumps nervously to his feet, goes to the window, and throws it open. As the noise of the crowd is heard more distinctly

CUT TO:

166. MED. LONG SHOT EXT. THE PLAZA IN FRONT OF URADI'S HEADQUARTERS
shooting past group at window. People are running from the streets that open into the plaza. They are con-

verging on one of the streets from which the voices of a growing crowd come over scene. We hear the shouts of those below the window.

CROWD (ad lib):

It is Benito Juárez! He is here!

CUT TO:

167. ANOTHER ANGLE GROUP AT WINDOW

The noise of the crowd grows louder over scene. Uradi bursts out in panic:

URADI:

Juárez must not come here!

LE MARC (anxiously to Uradi):

Mobs are always dangerous . . . Their moods are unpredictable. Give orders to disperse the crowd.

NEGRONI:

We shall have to use cavalry.

URADI:

No . . . Violence might call forth violence. The crowd must be dispersed peacefully.

NEGRONI:

It's impossible.

URADI (his panic growing):

I tell you Juárez must not come here.

CUT TO:

168. OVERHEAD SHOT JUÁREZ'S CARRIAGE

moving slowly in the center of an excited crowd. A line of soldiers with locked hands fails in its attempt to divert the mass into a side street.

CUT TO:

169. INT. URADI'S HEADQUARTERS

MED. CLOSE SHOT THE GROUP AT THE WINDOW

The noise of the approaching crowd is now loud over scene.

NEGRONI:

The crowd is still coming toward the plaza.

URADI (in jerky tones):

They must be kept off the plaza . . . (To Negroni.) Order your men to block all the entrances! Fire, if need be . . . !

NEGRONI (a little shocked):

On the townspeople!

URADI:

They must be kept off the plaza . . . whatever lengths we have to go.

CUT TO:

170. FULL SHOT HIGH ANGLE A STREET LEADING INTO THE PLAZA

choked with people, moving slowly with the advancing carriage. The camera tilts up to show soldiers with fixed bayonets deploying into lines across the entrance to the plaza.

171. REVERSE ANGLE

shooting over the soldiers at the approaching crowd and carriage. The officer in command orders the crowd:

OFFICER:

Halt!

The crowd halts and begins to pile up, thus checking the progress of the carriage.

172. MED. SHOT CARRIAGE

coming to a stop. Its door opens. Juárez appears in top hat, carrying his umbrella, a briefcase under his arm. Pan as he emerges and the crowd makes a lane for him toward the line of bayonets. It presses on close behind him.

173. OVERHEAD SHOT JUÁREZ AND FOREFRONT OF THE CROWD
approaching the line of soldiers, shooting from the crowd's angle, with a silent sound track. As Juárez comes nearer to the soldiers the officer's voice cracks the stillness.

OFFICER:

Ready . . . !

The rifles are canted to the loading position. The sound track cuts again. Juárez and the crowd behind him still come on.

174. REVERSE SHOT
shooting between the shoulders of two soldiers in the center of the line, to show Juárez only a few yards away and the crowd immediately behind him.

OFFICER'S VOICE:

Aim . . . !

As the arm in view commences to rise in response to the order

CUT TO:

175. MED. SHOT THE ADVANCING JUÁREZ
seen against the sights of a rifle, with the camera irised down. As the Indian's face grows larger because of his approach, iris up to include behind Juárez the faces of the crowd.

OFFICER'S VOICE:

Fire . . . ! (Iris down again to the sights against Juárez's face, and tilt the camera to show them wavering in indecision.) Fire, you fools . . . ! Never mind them . . . ! Fire!!!

(NOTE: The idea of this subjective shot is to let the audience *feel* why the soldiers did not shoot, by putting them behind a rifle themselves.)

176. MED. CLOSE SHOT JUÁREZ
reaching the line of soldiers. Their rifles are wavering. First one lowers, then another and another. The line parts before Juárez, he passes through it, and the crowd follows.

CUT TO:

177. LONG SHOT EXT. STREET FROM WINDOW OF URADI'S OFFICE
shooting downward over the shoulders of Uradi, Le Marc, and his officers at the plaza below as Juárez comes through the line. The crowd surges after him, engulfing the soldiers. As the Indian commences to cross the plaza with the crowd at his heels

PULL BACK TO:

178. INT. URADI'S HEADQUARTERS
MED. CLOSE SHOT URADI, LE MARC, NEGRONI, AND OFFICERS

URADI (turning from the window):

Call in the guards . . . Bar all doors . . . shutter the windows.

As Negroni and his men start to do so

CUT TO:

179. EXT. HEADQUARTERS
Benito Juárez at the entrance, knocking with the handle of his umbrella on the door. When no response comes, he knocks again—twice. Then, after waiting for a time, he turns toward the crowd and holds up his hand.

JUÁREZ:

Señor Uradi accuses me of misusing the extraordinary powers bestowed by Congress to establish myself as a dictator . . . He accuses me of sacrificing the cause of the republic to my own vanity and ambition . . . I have come here to confront Señor Uradi in the presence of you all . . . so that you yourselves may judge . . . Command him to come out.

A VOICE FROM THE CROWD (after a silence):
Uradi—come out!

Other voices take up the cry.

VOICES:
Uradi . . . ! Uradi . . . ! Come out, Uradi! (Mounting gradually to a rhythmic demand from the whole mob.)

180. INT. URADI'S HEADQUARTERS
Noises of crowd, shouts, rocks striking the shutters, and the thumping of rifle butts against walls over the scene.

LE MARC:
You must go out and confront him.

URADI (in complete panic):
I will not go out . . . Juárez will have the mob tear me to pieces . . .

NEGRONI (a little contemptuously):
Of what are you afraid, Señor Presidente . . . ? Benito Juárez is unarmed and alone . . . (He glances around at the other junior officers present. They look at one another and commence to close in.)

CUT TO:

181. EXT. URADI'S HEADQUARTERS
MED. LONG SHOT THE RAGING CROWD
Juárez still standing on a lower step. Rocks are raining against the building, and the shutters are splintering. The camera moves to a

182–83. MED. SHOT JUÁREZ
His back is to the camera as the door opens and Uradi appears, followed by Negroni and the staff officers. Le Marc comes out, but he hangs back of the group.

JUÁREZ:
Señor Uradi, I have come here to denounce you as a traitor before the people whom you have deceived

. . . You have conspired with Señor Montares and his landowners to betray the republic . . . You are receiving their support And the price you have agreed to pay is the lands of the peons.

A murmur rises from the crowd.

URADI (in a desperate effort):

He lies, amigos . . . It is a trick . . . What proof has he to offer?

As Juárez crosses toward Uradi and his group and stops some distance from them, the rest of the mob crowds into the room, climbing on chairs and tables and other vantage points to watch the proceedings.

CUT TO:

183A. CLOSER SHOT JUÁREZ, URADI, AND GROUP

Juárez raises his hand to silence the crowd and then turns to address Uradi:

JUÁREZ:

Señor Uradi—you have accused me of abusing the confidence of the people by wanting to make myself a dictator . . . You have accused me of sacrificing the cause of the republic to my own vanity and selfish ambitions.

Uradi, desperately trying to get hold of himself, stalls with:

URADI:

I have accused you only of what is self-evident, Benito Juárez.

JUÁREZ:

In what way have I ever acted as a dictator?

URADI (deliberately technical):

By decreeing to yourself an extension of the term of your office beyond the legal period authorized by the Congress when it conferred plenary powers upon you.

JUÁREZ:

In simpler words, señor, you mean that Congress did not want me to go on being president after I had finished my regular term of office?

URADI:

If you wish to put it so—yes.

JUÁREZ:

And you protested my doing so only because of your honest desire to defend the people against a violation of the Constitution . . . ?

URADI:

I shall always defend the people against any act of usurpation.

JUÁREZ (glances past Uradi and then continues almost casually):

And do I see behind you another benefactor of our people—Señor Le Marc of New Orleans?

CUT TO:

183B. MED. CLOSE SHOT A DOOR

directly behind Uradi and his group. Le Marc stands near it, a little uncomfortable at having been caught by Juárez as he was about to slip through the door.

CUT TO:

183C. ANOTHER ANGLE JUÁREZ, LE MARC, AND GROUP

JUÁREZ (to Le Marc):

Your presence here, señor, implies that your Society of the Friends of Mexican Democracy considers Señor Uradi the constitutional president of Mexico?

LE MARC:

That was decided only after careful consideration of the issues involved.

JUÁREZ:

And you have come here to turn over to Señor Uradi the current contribution from your society of two hundred thousand pesos which ordinarily would have been paid over to me?

LE MARC:
Yes.

JUÁREZ:
I see . . . (Then turning casually to Negroni.) General Negroni, when did Señor Le Marc arrive here in Matamoros?

NEGRONI:
The day before yesterday.

JUÁREZ:
The day before yesterday. That would be on the twelfth. (Then to Le Marc.) Then if your journey from New Orleans consumed the usual six days, that would place your departure from there on the sixth?

LE MARC (hesitantly; not sure of what he is driving at):
Yes . . .

JUÁREZ:
But the manifesto in which Señor Uradi declared himself the legal president was not issued until the tenth.

Le Marc fumbles for the answer to that one. Uradi tries to cover quickly.

URADI:
I naturally had informed Señor Le Marc of my intentions.

JUÁREZ (leading him on):
So he could consult with the members of his society and get their endorsement?

URADI:
Certainly.

JUÁREZ:

And he was able to do all that while he was on the boat en route here from New Orleans?

It is Uradi's turn to fumble. Le Marc tries to cover for him.

LE MARC:

What His Excellency meant was that he had consulted with me previous to my departure.

JUÁREZ (nailing him):

So that you, in turn, could consult with Señor José Montares of Mexico City . . .

LE MARC (not too convincingly):

That's a lie!

The crowd begins to repeat Montares's name. Uradi cringes under their steady stares.

JUÁREZ (taking from his pocket the report given to him by Tejada):

The United States government does not lie, Señor Le Marc. This report of its investigators proves that your organization exists only on paper and that all monies for its support came from Señor José Montares. (The crowd murmurs Montares's name with growing suspicion and indignation. Juárez turns on Uradi.) Señor Uradi, I denounce you as a traitor before the people whom you have deceived . . . You have conspired with Señor Montares and the Conservative Party to betray the republic . . . You are receiving their support . . . And the price you have agreed to pay for it is the lands of the people.

URADI (desperately):

He lies! It is a trick, amigos! He has come here with forged papers to entrap you! What *real* proof has he to offer?[56]

JUÁREZ (turning to crowd):
The proof that I have come here before you, compañeros . . . For will you not kill the one whom you believe has betrayed you?

A deep silence falls over the scene.

URADI (sensing that his own or Juárez's fate is quivering in the balance; to Negroni and the other officers):
Arrest him!

But the soldiers make no move in the silence. Juárez stands absolutely immobile, but blind panic grips Uradi. He gives a series of despairing glances at those about him. And then suddenly he snatches a pistol from under his coat. But from the front row of the crowd a big Indian takes a single step forward and whips a knife from his fingertips at the Spaniard. Uradi's pistol drops, his hands close over his belly, and he sinks slowly to the ground.

184. CLOSE-UP JUÁREZ
looking down at the dead man with an imperturbable stare. Over the scene is a roar of "Viva Juárez!"

PULL BACK TO:

185. FULL SHOT THE SHOUTING CROWD
and

FADE OUT

186. OMITTED

187. INT. DRAWING ROOM OF A HOTEL SUITE DAY
Although spacious and luxuriously furnished, the chamber denotes itself as a place of transient public residence. Through its windows the signs of tradesmen are visible on the buildings across the street. Carlotta walks up and down the room in a highly emotional state, which is not, however, immediately recognizable as rage. A door opens and her lady-in-waiting appears.

COUNTESS KOLLONITZ:

His Highness the Austrian Ambassador!

CARLOTTA:

How good of you to come so quickly, Prince Metternich.

METTERNICH (kissing her hand):

It is the privilege of a Metternich to serve Your Majesty's house.

CARLOTTA (freezing anew in resentment):

Can you explain the reason for the intolerable humiliation to which I have been subjected? Although I notified the emperor Napoleon of my arrival from the port of Saint-Nazaire, upon reaching Paris there was no one to receive me—not an equerry, not so much as a carriage awaiting!—and I was compelled to proceed with my suite . . . (she gestures in contempt) to a public hostelry.

METTERNICH (incredulously):

And you have heard nothing from the palace since your arrival?

CARLOTTA:

Nothing . . . ! What does it mean . . . ? I am Empress of Mexico . . . Why was I not received in state . . . ? Why was I not provided with a sovereign's escort of the imperial guard . . . ? Why was a palace not placed at my disposal?

METTERNICH (shaking his head):

I am afraid that Your Majesty's arrival in Paris is a serious embarrassment to the emperor Napoleon . . . His political situation at the moment is one of grave uncertainty . . . In Your Majesty's absence a new influence has come to bear upon European affairs. I mean the democratic idea. Power is passing into the hands of the people. Autocracy is being challenged.

CARLOTTA:

But what has that got to do with Mexico?

METTERNICH:

Everything, Your Majesty. (Shaking his head.) Because the sympathies of the democratic masses are with Benito Juárez.

CARLOTTA (shocked):

With Benito Juárez—I do not believe it! (There is a knock at the door and Kollonitz appears.) Our instructions were that we should not be disturbed . . .

KOLLONITZ:

I beg Your Majesty's pardon, but the Empress of France is here.

METTERNICH:

I shall await until she has left . . . We shall then be able to decide on a course of action.

CARLOTTA:

You are very kind, Prince Metternich . . . (She gestures to a side door in the suite. He bows and exits. Then to Kollonitz.) We shall receive Her Majesty.

CUT TO:

188. MED. SHOT

Carlotta at the head of the hotel's main stairway, her face showing mingled emotions of expectancy, anxiety, and hope. Two ladies-in-waiting are seen in rear. As a voice sounds, "Her Majesty the Empress of France," over the scene, Carlotta descends *one* step.

CUT TO:

189. REVERSE ANGLE

Eugenie mounting the steps with two maids of honor behind her. A respectful crowd can be seen in foyer.

EUGENIE:

My dear . . . ! It's such a delightful surprise . . .

(Embracing her and speaking in a shrill tone for the benefit of the assembly.) I cannot wait to hear all about your life in Mexico. What a colorful court it must be. Oh, it's ever so flattering to let me have a glimpse of you before you proceed on to Brussels. I'd be selfish and urge you to remain, but I realize you must pay your respects to your relatives. (Pull back and dolly with the pair as they move along a corridor.) Imagine my chamberlain, the escort, and carriages going to the wrong railroad station to receive you. How can I ever explain anything so absurd?

CARLOTTA (now realizing with what she has to contend):
Explanations are unnecessary.

CUT TO:

190. MED. SHOT INT. HOTEL DRAWING ROOM

Eugenie and Carlotta enter alone. As the door is closed behind them:

EUGENIE (brushing it aside):
And Max'l . . . Dear Max'l, is he as handsome as ever? You *are* fortunate, Charlotte. What a romantic pair you make . . . (Sighing deeply as they sit down on a settee.) Louis—poor Louis is ill again . . . devastated that he will be unable to see you before you return from Brussels . . . and Vienna, too, no doubt.

CARLOTTA:
It is not my intention to proceed elsewhere before seeing His Majesty.

EUGENIE (seriously):
Charlotte, his condition is much worse than we are giving out.

CARLOTTA:
Even so, he must be able to give me a brief audience. I have come a long way.

EUGENIE:

But he's dreadfully infectious . . . Really, it's quite impossible.

191. CLOSE-UP CARLOTTA

CARLOTTA:

I am going to see him tomorrow, if I have to break in.

CUT TO:

192. TWO-SHOT

EUGENIE (laughing it off):

Simply imagine . . . ! My dear, if you feel you *must* see Louis, of course you shall—as soon as he can raise his head. But now I must be getting back to the palace to look after him . . . If there's anything I can do to make your stay more pleasant, you won't hesitate, of course . . . Au revoir, Charlotte. (Eugenie imprints a kiss upon Carlotta's unresponsive cheek.)

CARLOTTA (as they rise):

Au revoir, Your Majesty.[57]

DISSOLVE TO:

193. FULL SHOT COUNCIL CHAMBER IN THE TUILERIES
with Napoleon, Eugenie, de Morny, Randon, Fould, de Lhuys, etc., at the table as in the opening scene of the script.

EUGENIE:

She will never be persuaded to leave Paris, Louis . . .

NAPOLEON (to Eugenie):

We are setting on a powder magazine, Madame . . . Her presence here is an incredible menace . . . If the public learn the truth about Mexico now, there will be barricades in the street.

FOULD:

Who'd have dreamed she would have landed in France without any warning . . .

DE MORNY:

It is part of her design to take us by surprise.

NAPOLEON (grimly):

She must be kept out of the public eye at all costs . . . Until she can be induced to proceed to her brother at Brussels, or to the Austrian court, or wherever . . .

EUGENIE (in sudden realization):

Louis—it is you and I who must leave . . . immediately! . . . before she can present herself for an audience. Then there will be no excuse for her remaining or publishing the purpose of her mission.

NAPOLEON (nodding):

You are right.

EUGENIE (to de Morny):

Arrange for a bulletin in the Court Gazette, M'sieu le Duc, advising that His Majesty left for Vichy this afternoon—at the insistence of his physicians.

NAPOLEON (coughing heavily):

For an indefinite stay, de Morny.

At this moment a commotion sounds outside the council chamber. All turn in its direction.

CUT TO:

194. LONG SHOT THE DOUBLE DOORS OF THE CHAMBER

flung open upon Carlotta, as she brushes aside the outstretched arm of an officer of the Cent Gardes. He, however, has sufficient savoir faire to cease his embarrassed resistance and announce:

OFFICER:

Her Imperial Majesty, the Empress of Mexico!

Hold on Carlotta as she advances slowly across the polished floor—in a mantilla, high comb, and full Mexican costume—to confront Napoleon III before the council table.

CARLOTTA (passionately):

We are here, sire, upon a mission which affects Your Majesty's honor no less than our personal interest.

CUT TO:

195. REVERSE ANGLE NAPOLEON, EUGENIE, DE MORNY, RANDON

This attack takes Napoleon completely by surprise. He conceals his embarrassment in a sickly grin, bows slightly, coughs, and glances toward Eugenie for support.

EUGENIE (stalling to recover her own composure, by gesturing toward the ministers):

The members of our council, Your Majesty . . . (getting hold of herself) who are here to discuss the Mexican situation—if possible, for the last time.

NAPOLEON:

Quite . . .

He nods to de Morny. (It is a signal for the duke to distract Carlotta's attention from himself. Randon takes the cue from de Morny and does likewise in turn.)

PULL BACK TO:

196. WIDER SHOT GROUP FROM CARLOTTA'S ANGLE SHOOTING PAST HER

DE MORNY:

We shall be pleased to hear in what way France can further serve, Your Imperial Majesty . . .

CARLOTTA:

Through living up to the terms of the treaty which induced Maximilian von Hapsburg to assume the crown of Mexico.

DE MORNY:

In what specific regard, Your Majesty, have we failed to meet them?

CARLOTTA:

By instructing Maréchal Bazaine's army to evacuate Mexico. Messieurs, you do not comprehend the situation. You cannot . . . otherwise you would immediately revoke the order of evacuation. The *Juarista* armies are all but defeated. Only a final blow remains to be struck. To avoid it would be a criminal waste of all that has gone before . . . plans, money, and lives.

RANDON:

I must disagree with Your Majesty as to the military situation. Our position in Mexico is exceedingly precarious at the moment. To secure it would require heavy reinforcement.

CARLOTTA:

Can it be you are not aware that Uradi and his followers have revolted against Juárez?

RANDON:

Can it be that Your Majesty is uninformed of the more recent happenings? (Carlotta looks at the soldier in apprehension.) Uradi is dead—killed . . . His followers have rejoined Juárez, who is now approaching San Luis Potosí.

197. REVERSE ANGLE (FROM THE GROUP TOWARD CARLOTTA)

CARLOTTA (tonelessly):

I do not believe you. (The marshal shrugs an apologetic shoulder.) If the *Juaristas* are at San Luis Potosí, more than the empire is in danger. My husband's life! (She moves toward Napoleon. In an awed tone.) And knowing this, you would abandon him? (She waits.) Answer me!

NAPOLEON (gesturing):

Regardless of my personal sentiments, as you see, Madame, I am in the hands of my ministers.

CARLOTTA:

In the hands of your ministers . . . ! Was it you or your ministers who conceived the plan to mask your infamies behind my husband's noble name . . . ? Who tricked him into accepting the throne by means of pretended plebiscite . . . ? Who assured him of French funds until the time when the Mexican empire could take its place among the nations? (She pauses.) Answer me, sire.

EUGENIE:

Your Majesty—please—you are overwrought.

198. GROUP SHOT CENTERING ON CARLOTTA

CARLOTTA:

Was it the names of your ministers which were affixed to the Treaty of Miramar? Did your ministers sign this letter? (She produces a letter and reads.) "I urge you to count upon my everlasting friendship. You may rest assured that my support will not fail you in the accomplishment which you are so courageously undertaking." (The sheet falls from her hand.)

NAPOLEON:

It is useless, Madame. Not another franc, not another man. We are through with Mexico.

CARLOTTA (bitterly):

You charlatan! (Taking a step forward.) What else might a Hapsburg have expected from the word of a bourgeois Bonaparte![58]

There are exclamations and a general confusion in the scene. Carlotta sways slightly and places her hands on the table. Eugenie takes a glass of water from one of the ministers and brings it to Carlotta, who waves her aside unheedingly.

CARLOTTA:

But you will not dare to let him die . . . I will drag down your empire if you do . . . I will proclaim your infamy in every court of Europe . . . I will denounce you for what you will be . . . a murderer . . . a murderer!

199. CLOSE TWO-SHOT

Eugenie, seeing a collapse is near, insistently attempts to force the water upon Carlotta. But something unnatural has come into the eyes of the Empress of Mexico. For a long time she stands in silence, gazing at the glass. Then her lips part slowly in the awed words:

200. CLOSE-UP CARLOTTA

CARLOTTA:

You are trying to poison me . . . poison me . . . poison . . .[59]

DISSOLVE TO:

201. MED. SHOT CARLOTTA'S PARLOR

The door of Carlotta's suite in the hotel is opened by a tearful Countess Kollonitz upon Prince Metternich. He enters in a hasty and excited manner.

METTERNICH:

How serious is Her Majesty's condition, Countess?

KOLLONITZ (sobs):

We do not know, Highness. We only know that she is not herself—not at all herself.

METTERNICH:

What physician is in attendance?

KOLLONITZ:

The court physician . . . but she refuses to let him touch her . . . or to swallow his prescriptions . . .

It is all I can do to get her to take a mouthful of food from my own hands . . . It is as though she were afraid of—but see for yourself, Your Highness!

Kollonitz crosses the room and opens the door of Carlotta's chamber for Metternich, who enters before her.

CUT TO:

202. INT. BEDROOM SHOOTING FROM DOOR

Metternich in foreground. Camera dollies forward as he goes to the empress. She is sitting, dressed as in the previous scene, with a handkerchief torn to ribbons between her fingers, in a state of utter exhaustion and apparent indifference. A faint quiver at the lips and a slight disarray of her mantilla impart a reflection of her mental condition.

203. TWO-SHOT

Metternich waits for a recognition, but there is no acknowledgment of his presence. After a few instants he disregards convention, bows formally, and addresses the empress.

METTERNICH:

Your Imperial Majesty! (Carlotta looks at him without interest and then resumes her former aimless gaze. Concealing his emotion, the prince continues.) It is I, Your Majesty, Prince Metternich!

204. CLOSE-UP CARLOTTA

CARLOTTA (consciousness dawning in her eyes at the sound of the name):

Metternich . . . Prince Metternich . . . help me. They want to kill me.

205. TWO-SHOT

METTERNICH:

Who wants to do such a thing?

CARLOTTA:
He.

METTERNICH:
Who is he, Your Majesty?

CARLOTTA:
The evil one . . . He is trying to poison me . . .

METTERNICH:
But why, Your Majesty?

206. CLOSE-UP CARLOTTA

CARLOTTA:
Because he is afraid I will tell his real name . . . People think he is an emperor because he wears a crown on his head . . . But I know better . . . I know he is Satan.

Camera pulls slowly back to a

207. MED. SHOT

CARLOTTA (her tone becomes confiding and childlike):
He hates mankind . . . His purpose is to debase humanity . . . to rob men of their godliness until they turn upon one another and destroy themselves like beasts . . . I must go quickly to Maximilian and tell him what I know . . . Only my husband has the power and the virtue to overthrow the Evil One . . .

Kollonitz, taking advantage of the prince's presence, enters with a cup of bouillon.

KOLLONITZ (advancing in the scene):
Your Majesty—a cup of bouillon . . . Please, Your Majesty . . . if only a spoonful.

At the sight of the food Carlotta draws back in some unidentified apprehension. Finally she raises a spoonful of the fluid toward her lips but arrests it in midair and lets it fall to the floor.

CARLOTTA:

Poison!

METTERNICH (to Kollonitz; shaking his head):

I will arrange that Dr. Riedel of Vienna is brought here immediately, Countess.

CARLOTTA (still staring at the bouillon in Kollonitz's hand):

You see, Prince Metternich . . . how he is everywhere . . . Every instant I am in danger until I get to Maximilian . . . (In the background Kollonitz begins to cry. Carlotta looks pitifully at the prince.) Help me . . . help me, Prince Metternich, to get to my husband.

METTERNICH:

I shall help you . . . Imperial Majesty.

FADE OUT

FADE IN

208. INT. MAXIMILIAN'S STUDY NIGHT

Dr. Basch is seated, smoking a pipe, while Maximilian stands before the fireplace. He throws his cigar into the fire.

209. MED. SHOT INT. STUDY

MAXIMILIAN:

Basch, I am uneasy about my wife.

BASCH:

Her letter when it comes will dispel all of that.

MAXIMILIAN:

The dream I told you about . . . last night I had it again. As before I was in the midst of darkness . . . smothering, fettering darkness. And out of the darkness her voice—or rather the echo of her voice—cried "Max'l . . . ! Max'l . . . !" as if in terror, over and over again. I answered, but she did not hear . . . I know she didn't hear—because the cries were repeated in the same tone of terror. "Max'l . . . ! Max'l . . . !"

BASCH:

A recurring dream, Your Majesty, indicates nothing more than a continued state of mind.

MAXIMILIAN:

It is so different from the dreams of her I had formerly. From them I drew comfort as from her living presence. Basch, do you know I could evoke certain scenes at will? In that subconscious stage before true slumber, I would envisage a certain setting then summon her image—as sleep progressed, the scene and her person would take on life in the reality of a dream, and we would kneel beside each other in chapel, ride together through the park, or walk by the pool at sunset. Then suddenly I lost the power . . . some three weeks ago . . . No effort of will could bring those dreams back. To take their place came this other—the dream in which she calls.

At this point in the scene, the beat of approaching drums is heard from the street.

BASCH:

If, upon retiring, Your Majesty will make his mind a blank—think nothing, as it were—but slip easily into sleep . . .

MAXIMILIAN (now hearing the stirring music of the band):

Listen . . . the last French troops are marching.

Basch goes to the window and looks out.

CUT TO:

210. THE STREET BELOW

shooting over Basch's shoulder. A French column in full marching order is passing, followed by a line of coaches.

BASCH:

And with them our first Mexican families . . . the erstwhile members of Your Majesty's cabinet.

CUT TO:

211. FULL SHOT A PASSING COACH
heavily laden with trunks and other baggage. Through its window the elegant figure of Señor José María Manuel de Montares is seen reclining against the cushion.

CUT TO:

212. CLOSE SHOT INT. COACH MONTARES
with padlocked coffers, jewel cases, and other packages of valuables piled neatly about him.

CUT TO:

213. MED. SHOT ROOM BASCH STILL AT WINDOW
Maximilian jerks a bell pull. A footman enters.

MAXIMILIAN:

See that all windows fronting on the plaza are immediately shuttered. Order the guard to let no one enter or leave the palace until the troops have passed. (Pause, during which the march swells in volume.) I hope I shall never hear that music again.

A footman closes the shutters.

CUT TO:

214. INT. NURSERY AT CHAPULTEPEC CLOSE SHOT
Shutters are being closed. Then we show Agustín kneeling beside his crib.

AGUSTÍN:

Blessed Saint Christopher, who watches over all travelers in peril upon land or deep water, preserve I beseech thee . . . (camera pulls back to show Maximilian entering to the child) the person of Her Majesty my mother and bring her safely home. (Bobbing up his head.) How soon *will* she be back, Papa?

MAXIMILIAN:

Soon, Agustín—very soon, I hope.

AGUSTÍN (getting into the crib):

I shall be glad, Papa . . .

MAXIMILIAN:

Do you miss her very much?

AGUSTÍN:

Mama played with me.

MAXIMILIAN:

I shall play with you tomorrow. Now go to sleep.

Maximilian hands him a woolly rabbit from the floor. Agustín puts it under an arm. Maximilian tucks the bedclothes around him.

AGUSTÍN:

Don't forget tomorrow, Papa . . .

MAXIMILIAN:

I won't forget, Agustín. God bless you. Good night. (He blows out the candle and exits, closing the door quietly behind him.)[60]

CUT TO:

215. INT. MAXIMILIAN'S STUDY

as Maximilian enters. Basch is seated as before.

MAXIMILIAN:

Poor little Agustín—he's lonely . . . quite lost without Her Majesty.

BASCH:

As are we all.

MAXIMILIAN:

I cannot understand why there was no letter from her by the last post. It is not like Her Majesty.

EQUERRY:

Maréchal Bazaine is here . . .

MAXIMILIAN (furious):

Maréchal Bazaine . . . ! Did I not give instructions that no one was to be admitted to the palace?

EQUERRY:

The commander of the guard did not dare to refuse him admission, Imperial Majesty.

MAXIMILIAN:

Inform the maréchal that we shall not receive him.

EQUERRY:

Yes, Imperial Majesty. (Exits.)

MAXIMILIAN (pacing):

It is cold in this room, Basch.

BASCH:

Shall I light the fire, Your Majesty?

MAXIMILIAN:

If you please . . .

There is a sound of voices without and the door of the room opens. Maréchal Bazaine enters in full marching order, with the protesting equerry in rear.

BAZAINE (saluting with a clash of spurs):

I am intruding against Your Majesty's orders. Very well, I am intruding. But it is my duty.

MAXIMILIAN (livid):

Then discharge your duty, M'sieu le Maréchal, as briefly as possible.

BAZAINE:

By the post which arrived from Veracruz today, I have received dispatches from the emperor Napoleon. He instructs me to impress the danger of the present situation upon Your Majesty and to beg a reconsideration of Your Majesty's refusal to withdraw from Mexico under the protection of French forces.

MAXIMILIAN:

We are not interested in any communication from the emperor of the French. Is that all?

BAZAINE:

Yes, Your Majesty.

MAXIMILIAN:

You have our permission to withdraw.

BAZAINE:

Your Majesty, forget if you can all personal resentments. Take my advice for what it is worth. I tell you as a soldier that your fight is lost . . . abdicate!

MAXIMILIAN:

Our decision is irrevocable, M'sieu le Maréchal.

BAZAINE:

But what reason is there for remaining when the outcome is inevitable? Four enemy armies are converging on you. All that will remain between them and the capital when we are gone are your native Mexican brigades . . . The empire is doomed, Your Majesty.

MAXIMILIAN (cutting him short):

We shall not attempt to explain our reasons for remaining here.

BAZAINE (studies Maximilian with something akin to regret, then salutes):

Adieu . . . Your Imperial Majesty.

Maximilian stands watching the maréchal as he leaves without a response to the farewell. When the door has closed, he goes quickly to a bellpull and jerks it.

MAXIMILIAN:

Did you hear, Basch—the post has arrived. (To the appearing equerry.) Have the post brought to me immediately!

BASCH:

At the risk of offending, it is my hope that the empress's letter may bring further influence to bear upon Your Majesty toward abandoning this unhappy venture.

MAXIMILIAN:

It is my duty to remain, Basch, and no earthly consideration can swerve me from it.

The equerry comes into the room with a sheaf of letters, which he sets down on a table. Maximilian picks up the post and swiftly scans it.

MAXIMILIAN (shocked):

There is nothing here from Her Majesty. (He goes through the envelopes again.)

CUT TO:

216. INSERT ENVELOPE

bearing Metternich's name as Austrian ambassador at Paris.

CUT TO:

217. CLOSE SHOT MAXIMILIAN

as he tears it open and begins to read. Over scene a crash of arms and a blare of martial music, which continues in diminishing volume to the dissolve.

CAMERA MOVES UP TO:

218. CLOSE-UP MAXIMILIAN

His face begins to reveal the contents of the letter. When he has finished it, he stands numbed, looking first at the front and then at the reverse of the sheet.

MAXIMILIAN:

Basch, have you ever heard of a Dr. Riedel in Vienna?

CUT TO:

219. TWO-SHOT

BASCH (unsuspecting):

Indeed! Your Majesty, he is the most celebrated specialist in mental diseases in all Europe. (Seeing the look on Maximilian's face.) What is it, Your Majesty? (As Maximilian raises both hands to cover his face the letter falls to the floor. Basch advances and takes the emperor by the arm.) What is it, Your Majesty? (Seeing the letter on the floor, he picks it up and glances through it hurriedly.)

MAXIMILIAN (lowering his hands from a bloodless face, he makes a desperate effort to compose himself, finally taking a step to the bellpull and jerking it):

We shall sail for Europe as soon as the details of my abdication can be arranged.

DISSOLVE TO:

220. EXT. THE GATES OF THE TOWN OF SAN LUIS POTOSÍ

CLOSE SHOT THE TATTERED FLAG

of the Republic of Mexico whipping in the breeze from the staff on the top of the arch of the gates.

Over scene comes a chorus of men's robust voices singing the *Juarista* march, accompanied by the brass and drums of a military band.

The camera pans down and pulls back so that in passing the top of the archway we see that it has been damaged by shellfire and are able to read the inscription on the arch that says San Luis Potosí. The camera continues back to a:

221. MED. SHOT EXT. THE GATES

We see a column of *Juarista* soldiers marching through the gates, led by a military band. The men, newly uniformed and well armed, are flushed with victory. They swing along singing enthusiastically.

Behind the column comes the carriage of Juárez, with Escobedo seated next to Juárez.

CUT TO:

222. MOVING MED. CLOSE SHOT JUÁREZ AND ESCOBEDO IN THE CARRIAGE

An angle from behind Camilo on the box. They sit, obviously a little proud of their victory, as the carriage rolls through the gates and continues down the street of the town.

The singing and the music that are heard over scene become less enthusiastic, then hesitant, and gradually die away to silence until all we hear is the rhythmic tread of the marching soldiers.

Juárez and Escobedo exchange curious glances at this strange happening. As they turn to look off toward the street

CUT TO:

223. MONTAGE SHOTS AS SEEN BY JUÁREZ AND ESCOBEDO FROM MOVING CARRIAGE

We see the desolation of a war-torn city. The street is deserted except for small groups of townfolk who here and there line the sidewalk. Gaunt, starved, and ragged, the people stand in grim silence that is almost accusing as they watch with apathy the arrival of their deliverers.

As the camera passes from group to group we see refugee Indian peon families pathetically clinging to their few belongings. The silence is broken only by the wailing cry of a hungry baby on the back of one of the Indian women. The townfolk are equally apathetic as they stand in front of their ruined homes and shops. Scattered among the groups are several wounded soldiers. One with a leg missing stands hunched on crude crutches. Another with a bandage covering his sightless eyes comes to a salute as the carriage passes him.

We also see apathetic people carrying away dead bodies that are still lying around. We see a mother kneeling in front of her dead babe, grief-torn. People come and pick up the baby to carry it away. The mother follows in stupor.

CUT BACK TO:

223A. MED. SHOT EXT. THE SQUARE OF THE TOWN

The troops who had preceded Juárez into the town are massed in formation before the town hall. Otherwise the square is empty except for the alcalde, or mayor of the town, an old man with a gaunt, haggard face, who stands with several other of the town's dignitaries on the steps of the town hall. They are dressed in threadbare frock coats, the mayor wearing the sash of his office. They wait in silence as Juárez's carriage comes into the scene and stops near them. Juárez alights from the carriage with Escobedo and turns to survey the empty square.

JUÁREZ (to Escobedo):
This, then, is victory?

ESCOBEDO:
It is war, Don Benito . . .

JUÁREZ:
Then it must stop—before the people of Mexico bleed to death of their victory.

As he walks toward the steps of the building and the alcalde and the others bow to him

DISSOLVE TO:

223B. INT. ROOM TOWN HALL

We see nothing of the room. Camera shoots over the back of Juárez onto the letter as he is writing. As the quill in his hand pauses we read what he has already written:

> Maximilian von Hapsburg:
> Once before I addressed you, telling you to leave Mexico. You did not heed my warning. Again I address you in the name of humanity, imploring you to abandon a hopeless struggle before the nation is devastated and drained of its last blood.

Then he continues to write:

> If you do not leave Mexico now, the guilt for that blood will rest on your head alone.
>
> Benito Juárez

DISSOLVE TO:

224. INT. STUDY

Maximilian writing at his desk. Prince Salm-Salm enters the room through a door in background. He halts formally and clicks his heels.

MAXIMILIAN:

Yes, Salm-Salm . . .

SALM-SALM:

The señores are waiting, Imperial Majesty.

225. MED. SHOT LITTLE AGUSTÍN IN DOORWAY

AGUSTÍN:

What's happening . . . (he looks around to see if anyone else is there, adds) Father?

MAXIMILIAN:

Things you will understand when you grow up, Agustín.

AGUSTÍN:

Aunt Josefa has come to take me to Washington.

MAXIMILIAN:

Yes, Agustín.

AGUSTÍN:

What is Washington, Father?

MAXIMILIAN:

A city where there are many big, white buildings.

AGUSTÍN:

Will you come, too?

MAXIMILIAN:

One day soon you will join Mother and me . . . (To sidetrack the subject.) But now . . . look, Agustín—

He stands Agustín on a chair at the table. On the table is a large package tied with ribbon.

AGUSTÍN:

What is it, Father—a present?

MAXIMILIAN:

Let's open it together and see.

When the wrappings are removed, a large and elaborate Noah's ark is revealed, packed to its roof with pairs of animals, to say nothing of Shem, Ham, etc. Agustín's eyes grow wide in fascinated excitement as the emperor sets the animals up in pairs on the table.

MAXIMILIAN (starting a giraffe's head into motion with his finger):

See how they work, Agustín . . . (The child keeps on looking and makes no answer.) You do it—to the hippopotamus . . . (Agustín stretches out his hand and barely touches the wooden head. Maximilian himself then sets it bobbing.) Isn't he funny—the hippopotamus?

Maximilian laughs. Agustín chuckles, touches the hippo, then bursts into a shrill of laughter. Suddenly Maximilian rises, goes quickly to the door, opens it, and beckons Josefa Iturbide to enter. She is an elderly Mexican spinster. He nods in the direction of the preoccupied child.

MAXIMILIAN (leaning down and brushing his lips against the boy's cheek):

Now, Agustín, take your Noah's ark and go with Aunt Josefa.

AGUSTÍN (heavily loaded with the ark and handfuls of animals):

Thank you very much, Your Majesty.

Maximilian motions quickly with his hand for her to leave with the child. When they have gone, he returns to the table and resumes his writing.[61]

CUT TO:

226. INT. LARGE ADJOINING CHAMBER
in which a crowd of better-class Mexicans are assembled, talking to one another in irregular groups. About half of those present are officers. From the study appear Josefa and Agustín and cross through the groups which make way for them by being appropriately saluted by officers and civilians. Colonel Miguel López comes through the company and approaches a doorway.

CUT TO:

227. INT. STUDY CLOSE SHOT MAXIMILIAN
as he finishes writing an act of abdication. His pen is poised to sign, when, hearing a step, he looks up with some surprise.

228. REVERSE ANGLE COLONEL LÓPEZ
standing silent at the doorway in background. The Mexican's face is a mask, which seems to conceal his torture of spirit.

MAXIMILIAN:

López?

LÓPEZ (the Mexican's great eyes regard Maximilian with the reproach of a wounded animal, as he speaks in a voice which is muted to a near whisper):

Is it true, Your Majesty?

MAXIMILIAN:

It must be this way, López.

López averts his face slightly at the words, closes his eyes. Maximilian rises, goes to the Mexican. Seeing that his cheeks are blanched, Maximilian is visibly touched.

229. TWO-SHOT MAXIMILIAN AND LÓPEZ

MAXIMILIAN:

Believe me, López, I shall never forget the faithfulness and loyalty with which you and the others have served me . . . never. (In an impulsive gesture Maximilian removes the Star of Guadelupe from his coat and fastens it upon López's breast. López looks down at the order and then covers it with his hand. Tears well in his eyes and course down his cheeks.) Good, faithful, López . . .

LÓPEZ:

Believe me, Your Majesty, I do not weep alone. Imagine, Tomás Mejía, the Indian—*he* wept. Does Your Majesty know what that means . . . tears from an Indian? Why, even as children they do not cry . . . Yes, Tomás Mejía wept . . . forgetful of his certain fate . . . only out of sorrow at his loss.

MAXIMILIAN:

"His certain fate"? What do you mean, López?

LÓPEZ:

Surely Your Majesty realizes what is in store for Tomás Mejía, for Miguel Miramón, for Márquez, for Mendez and for all others who would lay down their lives for Your Majesty.

MAXIMILIAN:

What?

LÓPEZ:

They *shall* lay down their lives. (Maximilian frowns in uncomprehension.) Does Your Majesty not realize what will happen when you have departed? Our cause will collapse for lack of the one person who can hold it together; without a cause there can be no unity; our forces will scatter, and Juárez will relentlessly pursue and find and kill each one of us. (The force of what López is saying begins to impress itself upon Maximilian, and seeing this the Mexican continues.) Yet in that hour—however far away from us Your Majesty may be—it will be some solace to know that it is for him we die. (Maximilian stands in troubled silence.) But, as you said, Your Majesty, it must be this way. We understand . . . your love for the empress . . . it is beautiful . . . Go to her with all our love.

Maximilian paces the floor three times back and forth across the room, in a dolly shot which is cut each time he reverses direction. López stands watching him, and a little smile commences to curl the corners of the Mexican's lips. Maximilian stops in final decision, goes to the desk, picks up the act of abdication, strikes a match, and sets the paper in its flame. At this moment, Dr. Basch enters, carrying a philtre of quinine and a vial of water on a salver.

BASCH:

Your quinine, Your Majesty. (Seeing what Maximilian is doing and realizing the significance of his action.) What are you doing . . . is it your abdication? (Maximilian does not reply but lets the flaming embers fall to the floor. Basch looks from them back to the emperor, and then to López, as if he were the answer.) What does this mean? Does it mean . . . ? (Breaking down.) Forgive me, Your Majesty, for my forwardness, but answer me . . .

MAXIMILIAN:

I have been blind to my true responsibilities, Basch. It took López, here, to open my eyes. (After an imploring look from Basch.) My love for my wife—(López's lips part at the corners in his catlike smile.)

Because of it I would have deserted the cause to which she has already given more than her life.

CUT TO:

230. CLOSE SHOT BASCH

BASCH (hotly and rudely):
The cause . . . What cause? It suited the purposes of others for you to think there was a cause . . . But one never existed except in your own heads . . . From start to finish you have been deceived . . . deceived by everybody—yourself included!

231. ANOTHER ANGLE INCLUDING LÓPEZ AND MAXIMILIAN
Maximilian attempts to wave the words aside, but Basch will not be silenced. He turns on López.

BASCH:
Bear me out, López. Has His Majesty not been deceived by everybody in turn? Are you not the latest to deceive His Majesty?

López's sad eyes only speak reproach.

MAXIMILIAN:
You will excuse the doctor for this exhibition of temperament, Colonel López. He believes he is speaking in my best interest. (To Basch.) Please, Basch, do not attempt to express yourself upon matters which you do not understand.

BASCH:
I understand enough, Your Majesty! I understand you are being induced to jeopardize your life.

CUT TO:

232. CLOSE-UP MAXIMILIAN

MAXIMILIAN (quietly):
Exactly, Basch . . . And is it not the sacred duty of a monarch, if need be, to sacrifice his life for his people?

CUT TO:

233. MED. CLOSE SHOT GROUP

BASCH:

Your people . . . ? What have you to do with these . . . (sweeping his arm) these cats of Venice . . .[62] You, an Austrian—a Hapsburg! Your single duty is toward yourself and the woman who is your wife!

MAXIMILIAN (withdrawing into his kingliness; icily):

Dr. Basch, you forget yourself . . . (To the Mexican.) Follow me, Colonel López.

Pan with the pair as Maximilian leads the way to the door in the background. As he throws it open

CUT TO:

234. INT. LARGE ADJOINING CHAMBER

shooting over the heads of the assembled Mexicans on Maximilian, framed in the open doorway with López behind him.

MAXIMILIAN:

Señores, it is our decision to remain amongst you . . . to seek a final and decisive action with Benito Juárez that will decide the fate of Mexico—and of ourselves—once and forever.

There is a rasp of steel as every sword in the room is whipped from its scabbard, and a great shout goes up.

ALL:

Viva Maximilián! Viva el Emperador!

At this moment Juárez's note of warning is brought to him. Insert it. Maximilian tears it up as the shouts continue.

DISSOLVE TO:

235. EXT. A ROAD IN OPEN COUNTRY DAY

Juarista infantry are halted along its side during a rest period in the day's march. Escobedo, Carbajal, and other staff officers, dismounted but holding the bridles of their horses, listen to a report from the coachman spy, who has encountered them en route.

COACHMAN:

His headquarters are in the Convent of La Cruz and he sleeps in a little cell. There is nothing in it to show it is Maximilian's except the picture of his wife. That is all I know, Don Benito, except that the soldiers say there will be no fighting until the army of General Miramón arrives.

CARBAJAL:

Good, Manuel . . . Get yourself some food and rest.

The spy exits.

ESCOBEDO:

Maximilian's plans are plain enough. He is waiting for Miramón to join him. Then he will take the offensive and strike at our armies in turn, as they approach from the east, the north, and the west.

CARBAJAL:

And if General Miramón's force should fail to arrive?

ESCOBEDO:

Maximilian would be in a trap. He is not strong enough to attack any one of our armies alone . . . But it is impossible to prevent Miramón's arrival from the south.

CARBAJAL:

You forget that Porfirio Díaz is in the south.

ESCOBEDO:

Porfirio Díaz has only a handful of half-armed peons. The fortress of Puebla and eighty leagues of mountains lie between him and Miramón's line of march.[63]

DISSOLVE TO:

236. FULL SHOT MAXIMILIAN'S ROOM IN THE CONVENT OF LA CRUZ NIGHT

It is a small chamber—formerly the cell of a nun—with a camp bed, a writing table, and a prie-dieu for furnishings. A portrait of Carlotta is in evidence. Maximilian is pacing up and down. Over the scene a bugle sounds "officers" call, and then there is a knock at the door.

MEJÍA:

General Miramón's army is entering the city, Your Majesty.

MAXIMILIAN:

God be praised, our apprehensions at his delay were unfounded. (He buckles his sword and picks up his hat.) Come, Tomás . . .

CUT TO:

237. EXT. A SMALL COLUMN OF MOUNTED MEN ENTERING QUERÉTARO THROUGH THE MEXICO GATE NIGHT

As it passes Miramón is recognizable. He has been shot through the arm and wears a bloody bandage. Almost all of the handful of men behind him are also wounded, some collapsed over their saddles. They are exhausted, dejected, and riding spent horses.

CUT TO:

238. EXT. GROUP SHOT MAXIMILIAN, GENERALS, AND OTHERS NIGHT

awaiting Miramón inside the gate. As the troops begin to pass between the group and the camera consternation is seen on the faces of Maximilian and his officers through intervals in the files. At a command, "Halt!", over the scene

CUT TO:

239. FULL SHOT TROOPS IN LINE WITH MIRAMÓN BEFORE THEM

attempting to salute the emperor.

MAXIMILIAN (to Miramón):

General Miramón . . . ?

MIRAMÓN:

I beg to report to Your Majesty that my command was engaged by Porfirio Díaz, and that these are its sole survivors.

CUT TO:

240. CLOSE-UP MAXIMILIAN

stunned at the words and unable to speak.

CUT BACK TO:

241. PREVIOUS SCENE

MIRAMÓN (dismounting painfully):

Díaz surprised us at San Lorenzo . . . and was on us . . . slaughtering us . . . before we even knew who he was . . . His advance guard is on our heels . . . a few hours behind.

MEJÍA:

A few hours . . . Then our line of retreat is cut . . . We are trapped!

As all look at one another in grim realization

DISSOLVE TO:

242. FULL SHOT HEADQUARTERS LA CRUZ DAY

The emperor, Mejía, López, and other officers are present. Dr. Basch just finishes bandaging Miramón's arm.

LÓPEZ:

We are surrounded, but the city is well fortified and we can withstand a siege for months.

MEJÍA:

Months of decimation and slow starvation . . . Let us try to cut a way out.

An officer enters the room and salutes.

OFFICER:

Imperial Majesty, an envoy from Escobedo has been brought here from the outpost line.

MAXIMILIAN:

Bring him in. (The messenger is led in blindfolded between two soldiers, and the bandage is removed from his eyes. All attention is centered upon him.) I am the emperor . . . You have a message for me?

MESSENGER:

Excelencia, General Mariano Escobedo demands the surrender of yourself and your forces.

MAXIMILIAN:

Upon what conditions?

MESSENGER:

My general demands that you surrender unconditionally . . . You are surrounded, and to resist further is useless . . . It is my general's desire that he shall not be compelled to destroy the town.

MAXIMILIAN:

Inform General Escobedo that I ask no conditions for myself, but that I shall never surrender unless immunity is guaranteed to my officers and men.

There is an immediate protest from the soldiers.

MESSENGER:

My general demands that you surrender unconditionally.

MAXIMILIAN:

We shall not surrender.

He nods to the escort, who blindfold the messenger and lead him from the room.

MEJÍA:

Assault, I say . . . Let us cut our way out.

LÓPEZ:

It is impossible—we shall all be killed.

MEJÍA (with a contemptuous look at López):
Some of us will get through, and those who die will die like soldiers.

MIRAMÓN:
It is not impossible . . . to break through. Resolute men have accomplished miracles before.

MAXIMILIAN:
Those below a certain rank have nothing to fear if we were to surrender. We have no right to sacrifice their lives in a forlorn hope.

MIRAMÓN:
They will gladly lay down their lives for Your Majesty.

MAXIMILIAN (after consideration):
Then let the men decide for themselves . . . It is my express command that they be told there is no dishonor if they choose to remain behind. Take only those who volunteer.

LÓPEZ:
I implore Your Majesty . . . What you are contemplating is certain death . . . There is a better way . . . If His Majesty and you others will shave your beards, we can attempt to steal through the enemy lines disguised as peons.

There is no response save sneering looks from the generals. One of them turns his back on the Spaniard.

CUT TO:

243. GROUP

MAXIMILIAN (shaking his head):
I know that you speak out of love for me, López . . . But what you suggest is not possible. (López attempts to answer, but Maximilian silences him with a gesture and turns to the others.) Señores, you will make arrangements for an attack at midnight.

MEJÍA (nodding approval; to a staff officer):

Concentrate every available man on the Hill of the Bells as soon as darkness falls, leaving only a line of sentry posts in the other sectors.

CUT TO:

244. CLOSE SHOT LÓPEZ
listening.

CUT TO:

245. GROUP SHOT MAXIMILIAN ET AL.

MAXIMILIAN:

Let us dine together this evening, señores. There are a few bottles left of some wine I brought with me from Chapultepec; we shall take this occasion to open them.

Over the scene comes the sound of a *Juarista* gun or two opening fire on the doomed city.

MIRAMÓN:

Escobedo's artillery—the bombardment has commenced.

DISSOLVE TO:

246. INT. MAXIMILIAN'S ROOM LA CRUZ NIGHT
The room is as before. Until mentioned later, the noise of a bombardment sounds over the scene. Maximilian, in the white uniform of an Austrian marshal, is standing before the mirror, pinning an order on his coat. After clasping the Fleece at his throat, he crosses to the table upon which Carlotta's portrait stands.

PAN DOWN TO:

247. INSERT CARLOTTA'S PORTRAIT
with several envelopes spread out nearby.

CUT TO:

248. INSERT ENVELOPE
inscribed Last Will and Testament of Maximilian von Hapsburg.

CUT TO:

249. INSERT ENVELOPE
inscribed To the Mexican People.

CUT TO:

250. INSERT ENVELOPE
inscribed For Delivery to Her Majesty, the Empress of Mexico, by Dr. Samuel Basch.

CUT TO:

251. INSERT ENVELOPE
inscribed To His Majesty, Franz Josef, Emperor of Austria.

CUT TO:

252. MED. SHOT MAXIMILIAN
standing looking at the portrait. As he turns and opens the door, dolly behind him into:

253. INT. REFECTORY
A spread table in the background. Miramón, Mejía, Mendez, Salm-Salm, Basch, and other officers awaiting the emperor. At Maximilian's entry they come to attention, with faces which express their surprise at his uniform.

MAXIMILIAN:
Good evening, señores.

Some respond with, "Good evening, Your Majesty," but others continue to look at him questioningly.

MEJÍA:
Surely Your Majesty does not intend to wear the uniform he has on in the attack?

MAXIMILIAN:
I do.

There are exclamations from the officers.

OFFICERS:
But Your Majesty! A white uniform! It will make

you the target of every rifle. Even if they don't know who you are, Your Majesty . . .

MAXIMILIAN:
Let us sit down, señores . . .

The realization of Maximilian's purpose in wearing the uniform begins to dawn on the others, and they exchange looks as they move to the table. Miramón, Mejía, and Basch sit closest to the emperor. Maximilian bows his head and says a grace before meat.

MAXIMILIAN:
Bless us, O Lord, and these thy gifts which we are about to receive through thy bounty through Christ, Our Lord. Amen.

CUT TO:

254. CLOSE SHOT TWO OFFICERS AT FAR END OF TABLE

FIRST OFFICER (whispering):
It is suicide— He wishes to be killed. (The listener nods.)

CUT TO:

255. MED. SHOT MAXIMILIAN

scanning the table. He notices that there is a vacant place.

MAXIMILIAN:
Who is missing . . . ? (After a look around.) It is López! (With some anxiety.) What can have happened that he is not here . . . ? Who saw him last?

MENDEZ:
I saw him in number eleven outpost about sunset.

MAXIMILIAN (to a servant):
Send someone to number eleven outpost to inquire for Colonel López. If there is no news of him there, ask at the field hospital.

The off-scene noise of the bombardment ceases.

CUT TO:

256. CLOSE SHOT TWO OFFICERS AT FAR END OF THE TABLE

FIRST OFFICER:

It is terrible to look at him and know that in a few hours he will be dead.

SECOND OFFICER:

Terrible . . .

CUT TO:

257. CLOSE-UP MAXIMILIAN

as he picks up his spoon but halts with it half raised to his mouth.

MAXIMILIAN:

Has the bombardment stopped?

MIRAMÓN (nods):

Queer . . . I wonder why.

CUT TO:

258. MED. SHOT COLONEL MIGUEL LÓPEZ NIGHT

coming through the darkness with three or four indistinguishable forms behind him. The sound of a sentry's challenge comes over the scene.

SENTRY'S VOICE:

Halt—who goes there?

LÓPEZ:

Colonel Miguel López and patrol.

SENTRY'S VOICE:

Advance, Colonel López, and be recognized.

Pan with López until he reaches the sentry, who lowers his rifle upon identifying the officer. The few forms in rear come up quickly. They are recognizable as *Juaristas*, and one of them strikes down the sentry with the barrel of a pistol. They then move on toward the city. Successive lines of *Juarista* infantry with fixed bayonets emerge from the darkness and follow them.

CUT TO:

259. CLOSE-UP RED WINE
being poured into a glass from a crested bottle.

PULL BACK TO:

260. MAXIMILIAN INT. REFECTORY
shooting past him down the table. He raises his glass.

MAXIMILIAN:

My comrades . . . Mexico! (He drinks.)

They rise in answer and shout in return:

ALL:

Long live the emperor!

CUT TO:

261. CLOSE SHOT MAXIMILIAN, MEJÍA, MIRAMÓN, BASCH
at the head of the table.

MAXIMILIAN (looking at his glass and turning to Miramón):

The wine is disturbed . . . Señores, when I came to this country I brought some Austrian vines with me and planted them at Chapultepec. This is from the first vintage. Are the Mexican vines flowering now, General Miramón?

MIRAMÓN:

No, Your Majesty, they were in flower a month ago.

MAXIMILIAN (to Basch):

But they are flowering now along the Danube. See, Samuel, it is the phenomenon you explained one night at Miramar—something of Austria, her sun, her soil, her seasons, will remain in the vine and wine from the vine forever.

Over the scene sounds a burst of rifle fire, followed by a shouting and a rush of feet in the street outside. A bell begins to ring furiously. There are more shots, shouts, and the shrieks of bayoneted men.

CUT TO:

262. FULL SHOT REFECTORY
as all spring to their feet. The door flies open and López bursts in.

LÓPEZ (shouting):
Quick . . . ! The enemy is below . . . Save His Majesty!

The officers pick up their weapons and follow López out at a run, Maximilian—a drawn sword in his hand—in their midst.

CUT TO:

263. EXT. COURTYARD CONVENT OF LA CRUZ NIGHT
shooting over a large circle of *Juarista* infantry, on the doorway. The Imperialists emerge to find themselves hopelessly trapped.

CUT TO:

264. REVERSE ANGLE
shooting from the doorway over the Imperialists, to show them hemmed in by the circle of rifles. They look around them in bewilderment. Mejía raises a pistol to fire, but Maximilian takes him by the wrist and draws down his arm.

MAXIMILIAN:
It is useless, Tomás.

CUT TO:

265. MED. SHOT ESCOBEDO
emerging from the *Juarista* ranks. Pan with him toward the group.

ESCOBEDO:
You are my prisoners, señores . . . Surrender your arms.

The ring of *Juarista* infantry begins to close. Maximilian nods, advances toward Escobedo, and tenders his sword—hilt first. It is ignored by the general. Soldiers disarm the officers.

ESCOBEDO (indicating the officers):

Take these prisoners to the rear.

As the soldiers begin to shepherd them away

PAN TO:

266. CLOSE TWO-SHOT MAXIMILIAN AND ESCOBEDO

MAXIMILIAN:

General, the officers of my following are guilty of nothing save doing their duty. I ask that they be spared all harm. If a sacrifice is needed, let the victim be myself alone.

ESCOBEDO:

I do not know you, señor.

MAXIMILIAN:

I am the emperor . . .

ESCOBEDO:

There is no emperor in Mexico. (Turning his back and addressing his men.) Let these two señors pass, compañeros—they are citizens.

PAN TO:

267. MED. CLOSE SHOT COLONEL MIGUEL LÓPEZ

standing nearby. Maximilian takes a step toward him as if to make sure who it is.

MAXIMILIAN (in realization):

You—López!

LÓPEZ (falling on his knee and grasping the emperor's hand):

Yes, Your Majesty. It was I who betrayed the city . . . (kissing the hand) to save your life . . . Come, Your Majesty . . . Hurry . . . Horses are waiting . . . Our escape is prepared.

Maximilian withdraws his hand and raises it as if to slap the Mexican across the face. But, at some second impulse, he refrains. As he turns his back on López and commences to walk away pan with him to Escobedo.

MAXIMILIAN:

Sir, I am Maximilian von Hapsburg, and I demand that you accept my sword.

ESCOBEDO (frowns and salutes):

Mariano Escobedo, Your Excelencia, commander in chief of the armies of the republic.

MAXIMILIAN:

I am your prisoner.

ESCOBEDO (taking the emperor's sword, turning, and handing it to an officer beside him who has previously been masked from the audience throughout the scene):

General Díaz, escort this prisoner to his quarters and set a guard over him.

Díaz salutes and leads off the emperor, with a small escort of men in rear. Pan with them past the figure of Dr. Basch, who stands watching in a doorway and

DISSOLVE TO:

267A. INT. JUÁREZ'S HEADQUARTERS SAN LUIS POTOSÍ DAY

The door of the room is flung open, and Mariano Escobedo enters the room carrying a sheathed sword in his hands. He is followed by Díaz, [Vicente] Riva Palacio, and [Juan] Corona. (These are the four army commanders.) Escobedo walks straight up to Juárez's desk and lays the sword on it.

ESCOBEDO (saluting):

Señor Presidente, I beg to report that the city of Querétaro has fallen and that the archduke Maximilian is a prisoner in our hands. (Juárez picks up the sword from the table and looks at it for a time.) It is the sword of the Hapsburg, Señor Presidente.

PALACIO:

It is the sword of a descendant of Charles the Fifth, whose armies first conquered Mexico.

TEJADA:

It is also the sword of a man who decreed that those taken with arms in their possession should die within twenty-four hours, Don Benito.

All eyes go to the Indian. Then slowly he lays down the sword.

JUÁREZ:

Maximilian von Hapsburg will be judged under the laws of the Republic of Mexico. (He pauses, and his own eyes now traverse the group before him till they rest on Porfirio Díaz.) General Díaz . . . (Díaz comes to attention with clicking spurs.) You will be responsible for the custody of the prisoner.

Their eyes meet. Díaz understands why he has been nominated.[64]

DÍAZ (saluting):

Yes, Señor Presidente.

DISSOLVE TO:

268. INT. THE STAGE OF A THEATER DAY

set for a court martial. A *Juarista* lieutenant colonel stands at the center of a long table, with three captains seated on either side of him. He is president of the court and about to read its findings. The defense counsel—two black-gowned Mexican lawyers—are seated at another table to the left, amid clerks, tomes, and inkwells. But a chair at the center of their table remains unoccupied. To the right is the prosecution table, behind which are several officers of the judge-advocate-general's department. What can be seen of the body of the theater is filled with citizens.

LT. COLONEL:

After considering the evidence and arguments in these proceedings, it is the verdict of the court that the accused, Maximilian von Hapsburg, is guilty as charged in count one, of having accepted the crown of Mexico from an unconstitutional minority . . . Is guilty as charged in count two, of having usurped the sovereignty of the Mexican nation . . . Is guilty as charged in count three, of having engaged in a war of conquest against the republic . . . Is guilty as charged in count four . . .

DISSOLVE TO:

268A. INT. MAXIMILIAN'S ROOM AT LA CRUZ DAY

It is the same chamber as in previous scene, since the emperor is held prisoner in his own quarters. He is standing by the bed, with a priest beside him, and Dr. Basch in the background. The cell door is open and through it a file of armed guards can be seen. Porfirio Díaz is in the entrance, continuing the reading of the verdict.

DÍAZ (in a formal, parade tone):

. . . of having procured the murder of thousands of Mexican citizens under his barbarous decree of October 3, 1865 . . . and finally, is guilty as charged in count five, of having combined with Miguel Miramón and Tomás Mejía, to foment and wage rebellion against the lawful government of the Mexican people . . . In virtue of which verdict it is the sentence of this court that the said Maximilian von Hapsburg shall be executed by a military firing party at dawn upon the nineteenth day of June: And may Almighty God have mercy upon his immortal soul . . .

PAN TO:

268B. TWO-SHOT MAXIMILIAN AND PRIEST

with the final words of the sentence sounding over the scene. Maximilian's face shows no emotion, but the priest's head bows and he weeps silently. As Maximilian puts an arm around the cleric's shoulder and commences to lead him toward a chair

DISSOLVE TO:

269. MED. CLOSE SHOT INT. JUÁREZ'S HEADQUARTERS AT SAN LUIS POTOSÍ

Juárez is seated at his desk, obviously busying himself with his papers, as Díaz, standing near him with Tejada, makes a masked plea for Maximilian's life.

DÍAZ:

Instead of the priest comforting Maximilian, it was Maximilian who comforted the priest. (Juárez makes no reply, but continues to work with his papers. After a pause Díaz tries again.) He prays that his may be the only blood to flow, and begs again your clemency toward Miguel Miramón and Tomás Mejía. (Still Juárez remains silent, but his face begins to show the strain of the intense struggle within him. Díaz starts again.) Señor Juárez—he told the priest he could look forward to death as a great relief . . . from things which he could not have found courage to endure in life.

JUÁREZ (rising to his feet, cuts Díaz short in a tone that is almost a cry of pain):

Do you think I *want* him to die?[65] (He crosses from the desk to a window and stands with his back to Díaz.)

CUT TO:

270. WIDER ANGLE

Díaz looks straight at the Indian. Then, without speaking, Díaz straightens and goes out through the door.

CUT TO:

271. MED. SHOT INT. ANTEROOM JUÁREZ'S HEADQUARTERS AT SAN LUIS POTOSÍ

In it are the members of the diplomatic corps, some eight or nine ministers, resplendent but distinctly uncomfortable and incongruous in their liveries. They watch curiously as Díaz comes through the door from Juárez's office and strides across the anteroom, exiting through another door.

CUT TO:

272. CLOSER SHOT THE DIPLOMATS

The Italian minister, losing patience, protests angrily as he glares off toward Juárez's office:

ITALIAN MINISTER:

It is fantastic! The whole diplomatic corps to be kept waiting like this for over an hour!

GERMAN MINISTER (a portly Teuton, as he wipes his red neck with a handkerchief):

I am wondering why you felt we should wear formal dress, Sir Peter . . . at such a time and— (he mops some more) in such a climate.

ENGLISH MINISTER:

Ah, my dear Baron, you Germans are inexperienced in the handling of native races . . . A bit of gold braid goes the deuce of a long way with these Mexican Johnnies.[66]

Tejada appears at the door to Juárez's office.

TEJADA:

The president will receive Your Excellencies.

As they move toward the doorway

CUT TO:

273. MED. SHOT INT. JUÁREZ'S OFFICE

Juárez, standing at his desk, bows to the entering diplomats, who mass themselves in a group before the Indian's desk, with the Englishman in the van. Tejada takes post behind Juárez's right shoulder.

ENGLISH MINISTER:

Señor Presidente . . . as representatives of the great powers of our European civilization, my colleagues and I have requested this audience to beseech you, in the name of humanity and of heaven, to extend a Christian clemency toward the person of Maximilian von Hapsburg . . . And, further, to offer you the assurance of our sovereigns—namely:

Their Majesties the Queen of Great Britain, the Emperor of Austria, the King of the Belgians, the King of Prussia, the Queen of Spain, as well as the Kings of Italy and Sweden—that, should such clemency be extended, they will readily give guarantees that Maximilian von Hapsburg shall never again set foot upon Mexican territory.

CUT TO:

274. ANOTHER ANGLE JUÁREZ AND GROUP

Juárez takes from his pocket the copy of the Black Decree, which he had taken from the hand of Pepe. As he unfolds it he speaks:

JUÁREZ:

Your Excellencies, I have here a copy of a document bearing the signature of Maximilian von Hapsburg. (Then as the diplomats exchange uncomfortable glances.) Did any of the monarchs of your European civilization whom Your Excellencies represent appeal to Napoleon the Third in the name of Christian clemency to stop the slaughter of innocent Mexicans . . . ?

ENGLISH MINISTER:

My government's expressed policy of neutrality and nonintervention precluded any action whatsoever in Mexican affairs.

PRUSSIAN MINISTER:

And I submit to the Señor Presidente that diplomatic recognition of a *de facto* government does not necessarily imply an approval either of that government or of the policies it may pursue.

JUÁREZ:

Your Excellencies make use of a jargon which was designed to conceal the principle that motivates your European civilization: a civilization which permits the oppression of the weak by the strong;

wherein each great power in turn inflicts its will upon some weaker nation.

CUT TO:

274A. CLOSE SHOT BENITO JUÁREZ
speaking out of the centuries, every line graven deep into his Aztec face.

JUÁREZ:

By what right, señores, do the great powers of Europe invade the lands of simple people . . . kill all who do not make them welcome . . . destroy their fields . . . and take the fruit of their toil from those who survive . . . ? Is it a crime against God, then, that the skin of some men is of a different color from others . . . that they do not wear shoes upon their feet . . . that they know nothing of factories and commerce . . . that there are neither bankers nor speculators in their land . . . ? By what right, then, do the great powers of Europe destroy them? If there is one among you who can answer me, I will give him the life of Maximilian von Hapsburg.

As he relapses into a stone silence

CUT TO:

274B. GROUP SHOT THE DIPLOMATS
looking at one another in the appalled realization that Juárez is making them endorse Maximilian's death sentence by their silence.

CUT TO:

274C. FULL SHOT JUÁREZ AND GROUP

JUÁREZ:

Then Maximilian von Hapsburg must die for a guilt that is not his own—but yours, señores—the guilt of Europe . . . The world must know that one generous in purpose was duped to his death by the vanity of power-drunk dictators, by the ambitions of unscrupulous statesmen, and the avarice of insatiable speculators . . . The world must know it, señores, lest those who duped him find another in his stead . . . The world must know the fate of *any* usurper who sets his foot upon this soil . . . The world must know that Mexico is for Mexicans, and not a spoil for the butchering, exploiting powers of your European civilization. We know that civilization, señores . . . for three hundred years we have endured it.[67]

Sir Peter bows in silence. And, as Juárez rises to return the bow, and the diplomats are ushered out by Tejada

DISSOLVE TO:

275. INT. CONVENT OF LA CRUZ NIGHT

MED. CLOSE SHOT MAXIMILIAN'S QUARTERS

The emperor is seated on his bed and Basch on a chair nearby.

BASCH (as he passes various items which he selects from a pile nearby—handkerchiefs, socks, linen, toy figures, sweets, and fruit):

Gifts from the people, Your Majesty . . . they pour in.

MAXIMILIAN (with tenderness as he takes up one of the crude toy figures):

They are kindhearted—the Mexicans.

BASCH:

Their sympathies are going to you, Your Majesty. Candles are being burned for you all over Mexico . . . Prayers are being said for you in all the churches.

MAXIMILIAN:

It is strange, Samuel, that I should achieve in death what I failed to achieve in life.[68]

BASCH:

Juárez will not dare refuse to sign the pardon. The people will demand it.

There is the sound of the door being unlocked. Díaz enters the room. He is carefully dressed and salutes with great formality.

DÍAZ (in a constrained voice):

Excelencia, it is my duty—to inform you that the president of the republic has refused to sign the pardon . . . that the sentence is ordered to be executed tomorrow morning at dawn.

MAXIMILIAN (anxiously):

What about Miramón and Mejía?

DÍAZ (shakes his head):

Their sentence will be carried out at the same time. (Maximilian, visibly moved by this, turns away. Díaz, who has been intently watching Maximilian, inquires of him.) Is there anything I can do for you . . . any request that is humanly possible to grant?

MAXIMILIAN:

You have already anticipated my every desire, General . . . (As Díaz salutes and turns to leave.) But wait . . . There *is* something! There is a song I should like to hear sung again . . . "La Paloma" is its name . . . Would that be possible?

DÍAZ:

Of course, Your Highness . . . I shall find someone.

They stand looking at each other for a moment. Then Díaz, afraid that he is going to break, salutes, turns abruptly on his heel, and goes out.

CUT TO:

276. ANOTHER ANGLE MAXIMILIAN AND BASCH

Basch can only stare at the complete composure of Maximilian, who turns to comment:

MAXIMILIAN:

So Benito Juárez is honest . . . If he were otherwise—ambitious, self-seeking—he would have set me free and won the plaudits of the world . . . But he is honest . . . My dying proves that he is honest.[69]

DISSOLVE TO:

277–79. INT. JUÁREZ'S BEDROOM IN HIS OFFICE AT SAN LUIS POTOSÍ

We see the room which is lighted by an oil lamp standing on the table. Juárez is pacing up and down, up and down. Then he walks a little farther than usual. The camera pans with him and we discover Camilo standing in the corner watching his master.

Camilo moves toward the window, and over his face we slowly see the dawn coming up. Camilo walks to the table and blows out the oil lamp. With a last look at Juárez, he slowly walks out of the room, leaving Juárez alone, who continues his pacing with the early morning sun slowly flooding the room.[70]

280. OMITTED

281. MED. CLOSE SHOT MAXIMILIAN'S QUARTERS

The emperor, with open eyes, is lying on his cot. He is wearing the same costume as in the previous scenes since his capture: a long-waisted, frogged, black coat and strapped, black trousers. There is a sound of footsteps over the scene. Maximilian sits up as the door opens on Díaz.

DÍAZ:

The singer, Your Highness.

He shows in a Mexican girl—a typical soldadera—carrying a guitar.

MAXIMILIAN (smiling at Díaz):

Thank you . . . thank you, General! (To the girl.) Do you know the song?

Díaz exits.

GIRL:

Sí, señor.

Maximilian nods and gestures her to a chair. He sits on his bed and looks away from the singer, who plucks a preliminary chord and commences to sing "La Paloma" in Spanish.

CUT TO:

282. CLOSE-UP MAXIMILIAN

with the song over the scene. There is an expression of groping—reaching—on his face.

CUT TO:

283. CLOSE SHOT THE SINGER

At the second verse (the verse of the dove)

CUT TO:

284. CLOSE-UP MAXIMILIAN

His expression has now become fixed and intent.

LAP DISSOLVE TO:

(Over the dissolve the sound of the song rising to a height, the voice fades, and orchestral music takes up the melody.)

285. THE OPEN OCEAN NIGHT

LAP DISSOLVE TO:

286. EXT. OF THE CASTLE OF MIRAMAR NIGHT

LAP DISSOLVE TO:

287. FULL SHOT INT. CASTLE A LARGE ROOM CARLOTTA AND KOLLONITZ

The music drops here and becomes almost indistinguishable. Kollonitz is tucking a robe around the knees of Carlotta, who is seated in a large chair. As the countess exits, the camera begins to move forward to a

288. CLOSE-UP CARLOTTA
Her face expressionless, her eyes staring straight ahead. Like one who has heard a faint sound, she turns her head very slightly, and the music begins to grow in clarity. Intelligence, comprehension, and finally joy show on her face. The music grows clear and true, with even a suggestion of the voice of the singer in far-off Querétaro.

LAP DISSOLVE TO:

289. EXT. HILL OF THE BELLS CLOSE SHOT DAWN
of Maximilian with an exalted expression on his face. The last notes of the song over him. Hold on him (Maximilian von Hapsburg in his long black coat, with the Fleece at his collar). Pull back farther to show that he is standing in the open air between Miramón and Mejía. Pull back farther to a full shot of the three as a *Juarista* officer comes into the scene tendering the bandages in his hand. Maximilian shakes his head. The officer bows.

290. MED. SHOT MAXIMILIAN, MEJÍA, MIRAMÓN, AND FIRING SQUAD

OFFICER:

Has Your Highness anything to say?

MAXIMILIAN (taking a purse from his pocket):

Distribute this money among your men, Captain . . . Ask them to aim at my heart.

The officer accepts the purse and salutes.

CUT TO:

291. CLOSE-UP MAXIMILIAN
The camera begins to pull back until Mejía and Miramón are included in the shot.

MAXIMILIAN:

Soldiers, do your duty!

The camera continues to pull back. The firing party comes into view, its officer with raised sword on a flank.

OFFICER:
Fire!

CUT TO:

292. PAN SHOT A FRIGHTENED DOVE
flying. The sound of a volley over the scene.

DISSOLVE TO:

293. LONG SHOT INT. OF A CHAPEL
shooting from over the entrance, at a coffin on a catafalque in the presbytery. A figure enters the scene and goes slowly down the nave. It stands motionless over the coffin. The camera moves up to a:

294. CLOSE SHOT BENITO JUÁREZ
looking down into an open coffin in which rests all that is mortal of Maximilian von Hapsburg. A look of pity softens his stone face.

CUT TO:

294A. WIDER ANGLE
Juárez straightens up and starts from the coffin, the camera preceding him as he continues up the aisle of pews. He passes an Indian woman who is kneeling in prayer. On her back, in the folds of her serape, she carries her baby, a robust Indian boy of a few months. The baby sucks on his fingers as he gurgles to himself. The camera stops with Juárez as he, attracted by the sounds from the baby, pauses to look at him.

CUT TO:

294B. CLOSE SHOT THE BABY
His velvet black eyes are on Juárez as his face crinkles into an ingratiating smile.

CUT TO:

294C. CLOSE SHOT JUÁREZ
The stone mask of his face slowly softens. For the first time we see him smile.

CUT TO:

294D. WIDER ANGLE THE TWO
Juárez squares himself and continues down the aisle as his short, squat figure disappears in the gloomy shadows of the church.[71]

FADE OUT

ALTERNATE ENDING

DISSOLVE INTO:

294E. LONG SHOT INT. OF A CHAPEL
shooting from over the entrance, at a coffin on a catafalque in the presbytery. A figure enters the scene and goes slowly down the nave. It stands motionless over the coffin. The camera moves up to a:

294F. CLOSE SHOT BENITO JUÁREZ
looking down into an open coffin in which rests all that is mortal of Maximilian von Hapsburg, Emperor of Mexico and Archduke of Austria.

JUÁREZ:
Forgive me.[72]

FADE OUT

THE END

Notes to the Screenplay

This screenplay is from the 1939 version of *Juárez*, which remains on only nitrate film stock at Warner Brothers Studios in Burbank, California. The version of *Juárez* now seen was reedited for a new distribution in 1952. Editorial comments in this script are related to the latter release. My sincere thanks to filmmakers Paul Stoudenmire and Matt Eisen for their assistance in evaluating technical aspects of the movie.

1 The prologue (scenes 1–29) referred to here does not appear in the film. It represents a belated attempt by the screenwriters to emphasize differences in background of the humble and "democratic" Juárez and the royalist, imperial Archduke Maximilian. Other scene changes were frequently made during the actual photographing of the movie as the writers sought to ensure audience appeal for the Mexicans and for hemispheric defense.

2 The Zapotecs are one of Mexico's numerous native groups, this one centered in the southern state of Oaxaca and noted for its magnificent ruins at Monte Alban, which testify to the greatness of their civilization about the time of Christ.

3 Now Ixtlán de Juárez, some twenty miles northeast of Oaxaca City.

4 Saint Stephen's Cathedral, popularly known as "Old Steve," lies in Vienna's inner city. Gutted by retreating Nazi Germans in World War II, it has been fully restored and today stands as the city's most famous landmark.

5 The film is in black and white. There was never any intention to make it in color.

6 San Pablo Guelatao is now Guelatao de Juárez (pop. 493), some thirty-five miles from Oaxaca City. The Palace of Schönbrunn on the outskirts of Vienna was the summer home of Austria's imperial court and the birthplace of Maximilian. Planned by a seventeenth-century baroque builder, it was reconstituted in the eighteenth century and remains world famous for its splendid gardens.

7 The Order of the Golden Fleece is one of Europe's oldest and most distinguished chivalric orders. Founded in 1429 by Philip the Good, Duke of Burgundy, its badge—a lamb suspended by a ring—symbolized the power of the Flemish woolen trade and was granted only to royalty and the highest nobility.

8 Bertita Harding wrote the book *Phantom Crown: The Story of Maximilian and Carlota of Mexico* (New York: Bobbs-Merrill, 1934) on which the movie is loosely based.

9 A Liberal majority in the Oaxaca state legislature in 1827 created a civil college, the Institute of Arts and Sciences, which attracted students such as Juárez from the local seminary.

10 Decades of domestic turmoil followed Mexico's break with Spain in 1821, as the nation's power brokers sought to determine who would rule and what direction the nation would take. The strife contributed to war with the United States in 1846–48 in which Mexico lost one half of its national territory to the victorious United States.

11 Civil War rent the nation, as conservatives railed against the new liberal (republican) Constitution of 1857. Meanwhile, a segment of the conservatives had already begun to search Europe for a candidate for king of Mexico.

12 Actually, England and Spain in 1861 joined France in the debt-collection venture, but on reconsideration they backed off and allowed France to pursue its imperialist designs alone.

13 Juárez was a nineteenth-century Liberal, not a twentieth-century land reformer. The Liberals believed in the sanctity of private property and sought to establish a countryside of Jeffersonianlike, small, independent farmers. They therefore decreed that the Catholic church and the Indian villages that possessed common lands called *ejidos* had to divide and to sell their holdings. Because of the domestic turmoil, it proved impossible to implement these changes, but over time through further legislation and unabashed manipulation much of the land was wrenched away from the Indians and to some extent the church and ended up in the hands of speculators and hacendados.

14 This speech is omitted from the picture, but Napoleon's remarks are noteworthy for the manner in which the screenwriters studiously avoided mention of the Catholic church in relation to Mexican land issues. To do so would have alienated U.S. Catholics. The movie begins: "I, Louis Napoleon, Emperor of France, pledge our wealth and the might of our army, not in a spirit of selfish conquest, but in a crusade to restore to our race and the rest of the civilized world, our ancient force and prestige! Let the world know that our conquest of Mexico is only the beginning of the fulfillment of our holy mission!" (see figure 1).

15 Translation: "Good God!"

16 One of the many ways in which the screenwriters molded history to

fit their story line. Napoleon did send his brother Louis to Holland as king, but Napoleon would have held Holland with or without Louis on the throne. As for Sweden, a French royalist, Bernadotte, assumed the throne, but he hated Napoleon and eventually fought against him.

17 President James Monroe on December 2, 1823, outlined the policy known as the Monroe Doctrine, which sought to limit European political influence in the Western Hemisphere. Monroe declared that any attempt by a European power to oppress or to control the former Spanish colonies would be viewed as an unfriendly act toward the United States.

18 Mexico was least indebted to France. Britain claimed $70 million; Spain, $9.5 million, and France, only $3 million, some of this last amount dubious. Britain and Spain at first joined France in its debt-collection mission, but they backed off when Louis's imperialist design became evident.

19 The Duke of Modena is not mentioned in the film. Instead, Eugenie suggests "the Archduke Maximilian of Austria! . . . Oh! But he's a Hapsburg, of course, and couldn't accept!" To which Napoleon III replies: "Not even if the Mexican people were to offer him the throne? Through a plebiscite?" The remainder of scene 32 and scenes 33–39 were eliminated as the filmmakers strove to both shorten the picture (which at one point was four hours long) and to lessen audience appeal for Maximilian and Carlotta.

20 Built by Maximilian and Carlotta, the Palace of Miramar lies on the Adriatic Sea near Trieste. Maximilian was a royalist without a court. At age thirty-two he was only two years younger than his brother Francis Joseph, the Hapsburg emperor. Next in line to the succession was Francis Joseph's young son, but the boy was ill, and if he had died, Maximilian would have become first in line for the crown, which he sorely desired. In order to accept the kingship of Mexico, Maximilian had to renounce his succession rights in Austria, which he did but then recanted, and a strident dispute with his brother followed.

21 Maximilian's explanation makes little geographical sense. By the time the Gulf Stream reaches Europe its waters are much-cooled. Water does vaporize from the Atlantic, but its effect on Trieste is minimal.

22 *Hibiscus syriacus*, probably native to China, is a common ornamental shrub ordinarily known as althea or rose of Sharon and thrives in any good soil.

23 Carlotta was the only daughter of Belgium's King Leopold I. At age seventeen she married Maximilian by family agreement, rather than love, although they learned to respect, if not adore, each other. She was a bright, cultured woman, but not normally so cleverly aggressive as portrayed by Bette Davis. Carlotta outlived all the principals involved in the tragic story of the French intervention in Mexico. She went insane while searching Europe's royal courts for assistance for her beleaguered husband, never recovered, and died in a Belgian castle in 1927.

24 Hofburg Palace, rebuilt and shaped for six centuries, was the imperial palace of the Hapsburgs in Vienna. Its stately apartments are now used by the president of Austria.

25 The Republic of Czechoslovakia was being dismembered in the wake of the Munich accords.

26 Audiences could interpret this speech as a reference to impending World War II.

27 This moral of the wine appears toward the end of the film at a banquet staged by Maximilian shortly before the *Juaristas* capture him.

28 The natural wealth of Mexico has frequently been exaggerated. Oil was not discovered until 1901 and did not reach significant production levels until the 1920s.

29 Such a plebiscite, rigged to ensure overwhelming support for Maximilian, was actually conducted by Mexican royalists.

30 The filmmakers inserted this letter sequence into the script weeks after the photographing had begun in the last ditch attempt to tie more firmly the fortunes of Mexico (meaning all of Latin America) to the United States.

31 Maximilian and Carlotta arrived in Mexico on June 12, 1864 (see figure 6).

32 There is no such thing as a zopilote vulture. The word zopilote means buzzard, more specifically a carrion hawk. Turkey vultures are common in Mexico.

33 Cortés finally conquered the Aztec Indians, rulers of central Mexico, in 1521 following a two-year struggle.

34 These musings on Mexican character were eliminated from the film.

35 Saltillo is the capital of the state of Coahuila below the Texas border. French military power almost pushed the *Juaristas* from their homeland into the United States.

36 Quetzalcoatl, said to have been bearded and fair skinned, was a Toltec Indian god-king expelled by competitors from his palace at

Tula, north of Mexico City, in about A.D. 999. As he sailed into exile from Yucatan, Quetzalcoatl vowed to return in the year of Reed I. That year coincided with the invasion of Cortés, and many Mexican natives apparently confused the arrival of the Spanish conqueror with the return of their god.

37 Maximilian and Carlotta remodeled and enlarged the Castle of Chapultepec and handsomely landscaped the surrounding grounds. A Spanish viceroy began the building in 1783; it fell into ruin after 1810 and was not restored for thirty years. It was used as a residence until 1933 and is now a major museum and tourist attraction.

38 This speech is not in the film.

39 This criticism of democracy was eliminated from the picture.

40 References to the letter that Maximilian found, the fake plebiscite, the negotiations of Bazaine with Juárez, and the maréchal's harshest comments about Juárez are not in the movie.

41 This outpouring of public support for Juárez was edited from the film.

42 Pepe's lesson to Juárez on guerrilla warfare appears later in the film (see figure 10).

43 This entire sequence (scenes 81–83) in which the duplicity between Montares and Uradi is explored does not appear in the movie, although later when Juárez confronts Uradi, the president refers to Uradi's agreement with Montares.

44 Carbajal's and Uradi's final comments are not in the picture, but at this point Pepe, the young shepherd from Oaxaca, gives Juárez the metaphor for guerrilla warfare.

45 Scenes 89–93 are excluded from the movie, including all references to the Society of the Friends of Mexican Democracy, an organization of high-placed Americans who schemed to take valuable Mexican territory in exchange for loans to the *Juaristas*.

46 Maximilian's favorable comparison of his ideals with those of Juárez were edited from the film, but theater spectators still blurred the distinctions between democracy and royal absolutism.

47 Costumers keyed the gowns of Bette Davis to her mental condition. When she was mentally fit she wore white, but as she descended into insanity her dresses changed to gray and finally black (figures 6, 7, 18, 20, 23).

48 Translation: "When I left Havana, no one saw me go . . ." From the song "La Paloma (The Dove)."

49 Agustín de Iturbide, a captain in Spain's royal army, conspired in

1820 with guerrilla patriots to win Mexico independence from Spain. Soon after, he had himself proclaimed emperor of Mexico, but within eighteen months republicans deposed him and wrote a constitution for the fledgling nation.

50 The entire sequence (scenes 134L through 134P) in which American speculators, including a U.S. senator, offer Juárez a low-interest, long-term loan of ten million dollars to sustain his fight against the French in exchange for a monopoly over all natural resources in the state of Sonora (across the border from Arizona) does not appear in the movie.

51 Actually, General Philip H. Sheridan was sent to the border, where he eventually commanded one hundred thousand men.

52 The *Juaristas* received no official military support from the U.S. government, although American businessmen and filibusters, sensing the opportunity for profit, eagerly aided the republicans.

Matamoros is situated in the northeast corner of Mexico, across the Rio Grande from Brownsville, Texas, and has always been a major port for legal and smuggled commerce.

53 Lane's meeting with Uradi is omitted from the movie. Instead, the scene shifts to Chapultepec Palace where Bazaine tells Maximilian that he has orders from Louis Napoleon to evacuate Mexico. Maximilian declines to abdicate, and Carlotta leaves for Paris to demand the continued military support of the emperor. Much of this is contained in forthcoming scenes 148–57, minus romantic details, which tended to create sympathy for Maximilian.

54 This entire sequence—the doctor's explanation that Maximilian "is out of harmony with his environment"—does not appear in the film.

55 Napoleon III ordered the expeditionary force home because of the threatening emergence of the Prussian army, which led to German reunification, the financial drain of his Mexican campaign, and U.S. diplomatic pressure (figure 17).

56 The entanglement between Uradi, Montares, and Le Marc (from the beginning of scene 183A to this point) is omitted from the film. Juárez simply labels Uradi a traitor, and the crowd gathered at the confrontation believes the president.

57 Scenes 187–92, which depict Louis Napoleon and Eugenie's attempt to avoid a session with the angered Carlotta, are not in the film.

58 In effecting his dynastic tie with France, Leopold of Belgium thought he had linked himself to the Bourbons, but the Bonapartes came to rule France and in doing so earned the Belgian family's antipathy.

59 Carlotta has gone insane (figure 23).
60 The departure of French troops from Mexico City and Maximilian's chat with his son (scenes 210–14) are not in the film.
61 This scene between Maximilian and Agustín is omitted, and as the movie stands, there is no explanation of what happens to Agustín when the empire collapses.
62 "Cats of Venice" is excluded from the film. It is a reference to Dr. Basch's earlier explanation of Maximilian's melancholy: cats thrive by the thousands in Venice (just as Mexicans thrive in Mexico), and one dog (Maximilian), normally the enemy of cats, cannot survive among so many felines, and so loses spirit and dies.
63 Scene 235 is excluded from the film.
64 Porfirio Díaz was not at Querétaro with Juárez. They had by this time become political rivals for the presidency.
65 The personal conflict that Juárez suffered in the script does not appear in the movie, because in the post-Munich international atmosphere, the filmmakers believed that democrats like Juárez should not allow sentiment to interfere with duty.
66 The English minister's condescending remarks are not in the picture.
67 This crucial statement by Juárez, which justifies the execution of Maximilian, appears in the 1939 version of the movie but not the 1954 release. European countries berated as totalitarian in 1939 had by the 1950s become Cold War allies of the United States and could no longer be criticized as imperialist adventurers. Germany and Italy, enemies in the 1940s, were the cornerstone of the NATO military alliance in the 1950s. So in the latter release of the film Maximilian goes to his death without explanation.
68 This outpouring of sympathy for the emperor by ordinary Mexicans does not appear in the picture.
69 In the 1954 version, Maximilian's remarks concerning the honesty of Juárez are the only justification presented for the execution of the emperor. Maximilian dies only because Juárez is an honest man.
70 And, it should be added, with a painting of Lincoln prominently displayed on the wall—Lincoln approving the nervous determination of Benito Juárez (figure 21).
71 This ending, scenes 294A–D, was rejected.
72 The comment "Forgive me" was blocked from the sound track on the film version released in Mexico, where Maximilian could hardly be forgiven for his intervention (figure 24).

Production Credits

Executive Producer	Hal B. Wallis
Associate Producer	Henry Blanke
Directed by	William Dieterle
Screenplay by	John Huston, Aeneas MacKenzie, and Wolfgang Reinhardt
Based in part on a play by	Franz Werfel
and a novel by	Bertita Harding
Music by	Erich Wolfgang Korngold
Dialogue Director	Irving Rapper
Photography by	Tony Gaudio, A.S.C.
Film Editor	Warren Low
Art Director	Anton Grot
Sound by	C. A. Riggs and G. W. Alexander
Costumes by	Orry-Kelly
Technical Adviser	Ernesto Romero
Makeup by	Perc Westmore
Orchestral Arrangements by	Hugo Friedhofer and Milan Roder
Musical Director	Leo F. Forbstein

Running time: 132 minutes
Released: June 1939

Cast

Benito Juárez	Paul Muni
Carlotta	Bette Davis
Maximilian von Hapsburg	Brian Aherne
Napoleon III	Claude Rains
Porfirio Díaz	John Garfield
Maréchal Bazaine	Donald Crisp
Alejandro Uradi	Joseph Calleia
Empress Eugenie	Gale Sondergaard
Colonel Miguel López	Gilbert Roland
Miguel Miramón	Henry O'Neill
Le Marc	Louis Calhern
Prince Richard Metternich	Walter Kingsford
Lady-in-waiting	Georgia Caine
José de Montares	Montagu Love
Mariano Escobedo	John Miljan
Dr. Samuel Basch	Harry Davenport
Achille Fould	Walter Fenner
Drouyn de Lhuys	Alex Leftwich
Major DuPont	Robert Warwick
Camilo	Vladimir Sokoloff
Carbajal	Irving Pichel
Riva Palacio	Pedro de Cordoba
Ambassador	Gilbert Emory
Lerdo de Tejada	Monte Blue
Pepe	Manuel Díaz
John Bigelow	Hugh Sothern
Agustín de Iturbide	Mickey Kuhn
Josefa de Iturbide	Lillian Nicholson
Señor de León	Gennaro Curci
Señor Salas	Fred Malatesta
Duc de Morny	Frank Reicher
Marshal Randon	Holmes Herbert

Cast

Baron von Magnus	Egon Brecher
Regules	Noble Johnson
Tomás Mejía	Bill Wilkerson
Negroni	Martin Garralaga
Coachman	Frank Lackteen
Tailor	Carlos de Valdez
Senator del Valle	Walter O. Stahl
Mr. Harris	Grant Mitchell
Mr. Roberts	Charles Halton

Inventory

The following materials from the Warner library of the Wisconsin Center for Film and Theater Research were used by Vanderwood in preparing *Juárez* for the Wisconsin/Warner Bros. Screenplay Series:

Play, *Juárez and Maximilian*, by Franz Werfel. New York: Simon and Schuster, 1926. 160 pages.

Novel, *Phantom Crown*, by Bertita Harding. New York: Bobbs-Merrill, 1934. 381 pages.

Research, "Some Notes on the Life of Benito Juárez," by Jesse John Dossick. No date. 179 pages.

Research, "Historical Period of Benito Pablo Juárez," by A. E. MacKenzie. August 26, 1937. 39 pages.

Research, "The Character and Career of Benito Juárez," by MacKenzie. September 10, 1937. 26 pages.

Treatment, "Phantom Crown," by Wolfgang Reinhardt. February 15, 1938. 141 pages.

Screenplay, "The Phantom Crown," no author shown. June 2 with revisions to August 1, 1938. 230 pages.

Temporary, by John Huston, MacKenzie, and Reinhardt. September 17, 1938. 165 pages.

Revised Temporary, no author shown. October 22, 1938. 180 pages.

Final, by Huston, MacKenzie, Reinhardt, and Abem Finkel. October 29, 1938, with revisions to January 9, 1939. 212 pages.

DESIGNED BY GARY GORE
COMPOSED BY THE NORTH CENTRAL PUBLISHING COMPANY
ST. PAUL, MINNESOTA
MANUFACTURED BY INTER-COLLEGIATE PRESS, INC.
SHAWNEE MISSION, KANSAS

Library of Congress Cataloging in Publication Data
Huston, John, 1906–
Juárez.
(Wisconsin/Warner Bros. screenplay series)
"Screenplay by John Huston, Aeneas MacKenzie,
and Wolfgang Reinhardt"—P.
1. Juárez, Benito Pablo, Pres. Mexico, 1806–1872—Drama.
2. Mexico—History—European intervention, 1861–1867—Drama.
I. Vanderwood, Paul, J. II. MacKenzie, Aeneas.
III. Reinhardt, Wolfgang. IV. Juárez (Motion picture)
V. Title. VI. Series.
PN1997.J78H8 791.43'72 81-50821
ISBN 0-299-08740-9 AACR2
ISBN 0-299-08744-1 (pbk.)

WW

WISCONSIN / WARNER BROS SCREENPLAY SERIES

The Wisconsin/Warner Bros. Screenplay Series, a product of the Warner Brothers Film Library of the University of Wisconsin-Madison, offers scholars, students, researchers, and aficionados insights into individual films that have never before been possible.

The Warner library was acquired in 1957 by the United Artists Corporation, which in turn donated it to the Wisconsin Center for Film and Theater Research in 1969. The massive library, housed in the State Historical Society of Wisconsin, contains eight hundred sound feature films, fifteen hundred short subjects, and nineteen thousand still negatives, as well as the legal files, press books, and screenplays of virtually every Warner film produced from 1930 until 1950. This rich treasure trove has made the University of Wisconsin one of the major centers for film research, attracting scholars from around the world. This series of published screenplays represents a creative use of the Warner library, both a boon to scholars and a tribute to United Artists.

Most published film scripts are literal transcriptions of finished films. The Wisconsin/Warner screenplays are primary source documents—the final shooting versions including revisions made during production. As such, they reveal the art of screenwriting as other film transcriptions cannot. Comparing these screenplays with the final films will illuminate the arts of directing and acting, as well as the other arts of the film making process. (Films of the Warner library are available at modest rates from the United Artists nontheatrical rental library, United Artists/16 mm.)

From the eight hundred feature films in the library, the editors of the series selected for publication examples that have received critical recognition for excellence of directing, screenwriting, and acting, films distinctive in genre, in historical relevance, and in adaptation of well-known novels and plays.